MAKING PSHE MATTER

of related interest

Character Toolkit for Teachers
Classroom and Whole School Character Education
Activities for 5- to 11-year-olds
Frederika Roberts and Elizabeth Wright
Foreword by Kristján Kristjánsson
ISBN 978 1 78592 490 3
eISBN 978 1 78450 879 1

Promoting Young Children's Emotional Health and Wellbeing
A Practical Guide for Professionals and Parents
Sonia Mainstone-Cotton
ISBN 978 1 78592 054 7
eISBN 978 1 78450 311 6

Implementing Restorative Practice in Schools
A Practical Guide to Transforming School Communities
Margaret Thorsborne and Peta Blood
ISBN 978 1 84905 377 8
eISBN 978 0 85700 737 7

Building Positive Momentum for Positive Behavior in Young Children
Strategies for Success in School and Beyond
Lisa Rogers
ISBN 978 1 78592 774 4
eISBN 978 1 78450 679 7

Lucy the Octopus
Richy K. Chandler
ISBN 978 1 78592 513 9
eISBN 978 1 78450 902 6

Life Coaching for Kids
A Practical Manual to Coach Children and Young
People to Success, Well-being and Fulfilment
Nikki Giant
ISBN 978 1 84905 982 4
eISBN 978 0 85700 884 8

MAKING
PSHE
MATTER

A Practical Guide to Planning
and Teaching Creative PSHE
in Primary School

Siân Rowland

Jessica Kingsley *Publishers*
London and Philadelphia

First published in 2018
by Jessica Kingsley Publishers
73 Collier Street
London N1 9BE, UK
and
400 Market Street, Suite 400
Philadelphia, PA 19106, USA

www.jkp.com

Library of Congress Cataloging in Publication Data
A CIP catalog record for this book is available from the Library of Congress

British Library Cataloguing in Publication Data
A CIP catalogue record for this book is available from the British Library

ISBN 978 1 78592 286 2
eISBN 978 1 78450 590 5

Printed and bound in Great Britain

Contents

INTRODUCTION

This book is designed with the primary classroom teacher in mind. Perhaps you're new to teaching or perhaps you simply want to gain a greater understanding of what PSHE is and what works or to brush up on your skills. Perhaps you're part of the middle management or senior leadership team. Perhaps you're thinking about leading PSHE in your school – while this book is not primarily about being a subject leader, it does look at some of the wider issues of planning whole-school events, and it touches briefly on planning and policy in order to give the broader picture of where PSHE sits.

Whatever your involvement in teaching PSHE, you'll find ideas, case studies and support to point you in the right direction and to spark some ideas for making PSHE teaching and learning meaningful, active and creative. A Year Six pupil once said to me, 'All we do in PSHE is sit around and talk about our feelings.' This book, which describes both familiar formats and more creative approaches, may inspire teachers with new ideas for engaging pupils' interest.

This isn't a textbook or a scheme of work, but it does include ideas for lessons that have been tried and tested in the primary classroom, and can therefore act as a starting point for outstanding teaching and learning in PSHE. While it may be tempting to jump to the activities section, it's important too to see the context properly, so we start with the wider context of PSHE and then gradually work our way towards planning and delivering creative lessons. Think of it like decorating a room: putting the wallpaper up and hanging pictures is the fun bit, but if you don't spend time in proper preparation the wallpaper is likely to start peeling pretty quickly!

There are case studies dotted throughout the chapters, which are drawn from practising teachers and from a few experts in relevant fields:

these give a practical context to the theory. There are also ideas for follow-up activities, things to think about, and notes on helpful organisations that can provide specialist advice and support.

Hardly anyone actually sets out to be a PSHE teacher, it seems, yet somehow the subject finds us! For me, being a good teacher is about aiming to give children the best educational experience we possibly can in order to help them take the next step of their lives with confidence. And that means finding a balance between offering the best academic teaching and learning we can offer while also developing the whole child. PSHE is unique in that it straddles both of these facets. It should and must be taught with aspiration and educational rigour, but it can also provide the best opportunity for children to explore and to develop the skills that will allow them to thrive in a complex world.

Bring to your PSHE lessons the passion you have for teaching and learning in other subjects, and you won't go far wrong.

Siân Rowland

Chapter One

LOOKING AT THE BIGGER PICTURE

Understanding PSHE

> PSHE education gives pupils the knowledge, skills, and attributes they need to keep themselves healthy and safe and to prepare them for life and work in modern Britain.
>
> *PSHE Association*

First there's the name. For the purposes of this book, I'll use 'PSHE' ('Personal, Social and Health Education'), but you may also see it described as 'PSHE Education' (with the second 'E' standing for 'Economic') or with an added 'C' (PSHCE) for 'Citizenship'. Whatever you call it in your school, however, PSHE includes the study of those elusive, ephemeral aspects of life that help children to thrive in a complex and challenging world. PSHE is an area of the curriculum where children can think, carry out activities, discuss issues and develop key skills in a safe environment.

But aren't such matters for the parent to decide? Isn't developing morals and values, and the skills needed to tackle the world, the very essence of parenting? Of course it is; but schools have their part to play too, and PSHE is one of the elements in a child's development. Helping a child to develop the skills to thrive is a privilege shared by all of those involved in the child's upbringing. PSHE is not a subject done 'to' children: it's the development of skills delivered in a cohesive way while they are at school.

Imagine it's the last day of Year Six. The children have finished their exams and assessments, the reports have been delivered, and there isn't a dry eye in the house after the leavers' assembly. What do we want those children going on to secondary school to take with them? Academic achievement, certainly. They need to be literate and numerate and ready for the next steps in their academic careers. But they need more: they need confidence to take those next steps; relationship skills that will enable them to manage changing friendships and their interactions with the many people they will meet; skills that will help them manage conflict and resolve disputes; the ability to make choices, to manage risk and to assert themselves; the ability to travel independently and safely to and from school; the capacity to make informed choices about what they eat and how they spend their free time; and they need to be able to communicate effectively. That's just the tip of the iceberg of skills needed to negotiate secondary schools and looming adolescence. We can trust that children will pick up some ideas themselves, and that parents and carers are the primary guides in supporting their children, but in offering well-planned, comprehensive PSHE sessions in primary schools we can give children the opportunity to practise and develop life skills in a safe environment before going out into the big, wide world.

In PSHE we often talk about a *spiral curriculum* – a curriculum that begins in Early Years and builds, grows and develops as children go through the school. The child begins with simple skills, practises and explores these skills, and then progresses and builds upon them. When schools say that they deliver their Relationships and Sex Education (RSE) in Year Five or Year Six, they're actually incorrect. We start teaching children about relationships as soon as they first set foot in school, as they learn to share the toys, to take turns and to make new friends. They start with age-appropriate skills, and these grow and develop as the children do. We'll cover more about the spiral curriculum later, but this and the *skills threads* together represent the core that goes through the whole-school curriculum.

This spiral curriculum acts as a scaffold which supports PSHE teaching and learning. Take away one element of the spiral and it collapses. You can think of it in terms of any other subject – Mathematics, for example. You wouldn't suddenly introduce long-division methods unless pupils already had a grasp on short division, had experienced this in both concrete and abstract forms and had practised doing some dividing. Only when they're ready for formal calculation methods do you teach them how, and then the pupils practise, you correct and support where necessary, and you assess progress. This takes time and probably can't be completed in just one session, and it's the same with PSHE. When a new topic is introduced, then it needs to be planned and taught effectively with the highest aspirations. The pupils need time and space to practise the new skills, and the teacher then needs to assess whether learning has taken place and what steps to take next.

PSHE may sometimes be seen as a desirable rather than an essential part of the overall curriculum. I would argue that PSHE should and must be at the *heart* of the primary school's curriculum. It can drive everything the school does and it can support and contribute to your school's ethos, to its Spiritual, Moral, Social and Cultural (SMSC) requirements, and to the wellbeing and happiness of pupils. Ultimately PSHE is integral to academic attainment too, so it can't be seen as something separate.

Children need to feel safe and secure at school, healthy and ready to learn. If they are in fear of bullying or have unhappy friendships, if they are hungry, sad or struggling with mental health issues, they will not learn as effectively as they could. Obviously PSHE is not the answer to all known ills (if only it were!), but it can provide a forum in which pupils can explore feelings, develop understanding and practise skills. It provides a time to explore and debate challenging issues that all children have to deal with.

The PSHE curriculum must be carefully planned to meet the needs of the children in *your* school. 'One size fits all' doesn't work with PSHE. You know the needs of your pupils best; whether your school is a small rural school with vertically grouped classes, a large urban primary with a transient population, or a single-sex faith school, PSHE needs to be carefully planned to address *their* particular needs.

Teachers often ask whether there's a recommended programme of study or a resource pack. There are such materials, of course, but you need to carefully select the topics you want to teach and when those will be taught. We'll look at selecting resources and schemes later on, but a good starting point is the PSHE Association's *Programme of Study*.[1]

The Association has broken down PSHE into three core themes:

- Health and wellbeing

- Relationships

- Living in the wider world – economic wellbeing and being a responsible citizen

---

1   PSHE Association (2017) *Programme of Study*. London: PSHE Association.

These three core themes are divided into Key Stage 1 and Key Stage 2. That way, schools and teachers can decide whether their pupils are ready for a certain topic in Year Three or Year Six, in the autumn term or the summer term. The programme isn't prescriptive and offers flexibility for schools to decide how and when they teach particular topics.

Starting with the bigger picture of PSHE and how PSHE fits into contemporary school life, we will then start to focus on the elements that make up effective PSHE teaching and learning, and how all of the threads can be gathered together into one cohesive programme. In order to have a clear picture of where we are now, however, we need first to look at the past.

Delving into history

Up until the 1990s, the teaching of life skills and health and wellbeing had always been a bit ad hoc. Although programmes such as *Jugs and Herrings* (a Southampton University study[2] into drug education in the 1980s) were being used in some classrooms, there wasn't a coherent approach to health and wellbeing teaching across all schools.

With the advent of the National Curriculum in 1990, however, the primary timetable suddenly got busier and became more focused on outcomes. The moments where class chat about wellbeing and special projects might previously have been slotted in were now being targeted for compulsory National Curriculum subject areas. Anyone who was teaching in the early '90s will remember the first incarnation of the Science curriculum, for example, with its 17 attainment targets, and the growth of Standard Assessment Tests (SATs) at the end of Key Stage 1 to include testing on History and Geography as well as English, Maths and Science.

PSHE as a separate subject area came into the National Curriculum as a non-statutory subject, but because of its prominence in the spiral-bound book[3] it was taken more seriously as a subject and local authorities responded by recruiting advisers to support schools with planning, training and delivery.

2   HEA Primary Project Team (1986) *Jugs and Herrings.* Unpublished study, Southampton University.
3   Department for Education (DfE) (2000) *The National Curriculum, Key Stages 1 and 2: Handbook for Primary Teachers in England.* London: DfE.

Around the same time, the Healthy Schools Standard was also developed, as a way of assessing, supporting and celebrating health and wellbeing in schools. This arose from earlier health-promoting projects in schools. Each area developed its own version of the Healthy Schools programme and many schools welcomed the support and structure it gave.

By 2005 the National Healthy Schools Programme (NHSP) had been developed and unified across England, with an award system for those schools reaching the National Healthy Schools Status (NHSS). Schools had to demonstrate that they had reached certain standards in four key areas:

- PSHE

- Healthy eating

- Physical activity

- Emotional health and wellbeing

The programme came on top of a public demand for healthier schools. Jamie Oliver's call for reform of school meals forced the government into action, and the NHSP helped make the link between making healthier choices and ensuring meal providers worked with schools, pupils and parents to improve school meal take-up.

New initiatives such as the Social and Emotional Aspects of Learning (SEAL) programme were rolled out to schools, with attached funding, and the PSHE Association was formed to support schools, teachers and practitioners. PSHE was still non-statutory and teaching and learning were still patchy, but many schools were committed to improving and were keen to attain Healthy Schools Status. Finally PSHE was being put on the map.

The status of PSHE was further boosted by the introduction of the PSHE certification process, a one-year course for teachers, community nurses and other professionals working in schools. Participants were able to gain a deeper knowledge and understanding of how to teach PSHE, and schools had access to well-trained members of staff who would champion PSHE in their schools and local areas. The certification process was rigorous and assessed by a range of external assessors; it gave participants a thorough grounding in teaching PSHE and learning through PSHE, and enabled them to support their own and other schools. The positive approach to joined-up services and support for children continued with the introduction in 2003, at local authority level, of *Every Child Matters*,[4] a government initiative that led to the Children Act 2004. The aim was to ensure that children's services, including education and social services, communicated more effectively with one another. Ofsted inspection requirements changed and extended schools services were introduced, putting schools at the heart of the community.

With its five themes – stay safe, be healthy, enjoy and achieve, make a positive contribution, and achieve economic wellbeing – *Every Child Matters* created a duty of care for all local authorities, which were required to say what they were doing in terms of improving health and wellbeing opportunities for children and young people. This put PSHE and Healthy Schools front and centre.

In 2009 Sir Alastair Macdonald published his *Independent Review of the Proposal to Make Personal, Social, Health and Economic (PSHE) Education Statutory* and a bill (the Macdonald Bill) started to proceed through Parliament.

Meanwhile, however, the global economic crash was beginning to bite, and in 2010 a General Election was called and contested. The newly elected coalition government called for cuts to the public sector, and these cuts included the NHSP budget, extended schools services and the successful School Sports Partnership, which had ensured that all pupils had access to two and a half hours of curriculum sports per week. As the carefully built infrastructure of support crumbled, PSHE once again took a back seat.

The Macdonald Bill fell through when the new government came in and PSHE was not included in the new Children, Schools and Families Bill. A new review was promised but failed to materialise, and the government, taking the line that schools should be autonomous in selecting a programme that worked for them and their pupils, focused instead on creating academies and free schools.

The PSHE Association continued to thrive, however, and as always led the way in promoting PSHE and supporting teachers. The Association came to the rescue with the introduction in 2013 of a

---

4   Chief Secretary to the Treasury (2003) *Every Child Matters*. London: The Stationery Office; Children's Commissioner (2004) *The Children Act*. London: Parliament of the United Kingdom.

new programme of study, thereby ensuring that schools had some scaffolding in creating a curriculum that worked in the context of a new technological world and a crowded timetable. The Association continues to develop key materials for schools, runs an annual conference, and has developed a Quality Mark for resources that meet the requirements for effective PSHE teaching and learning.

The government's Sex and Relationship Education guidance, issued in 2000,[5] had not been updated to meet the needs of modern schools, so in 2014 the PSHE Association, in partnership with Brook and the Sex Education Forum, stepped in and created a key document, *Sex and Relationships Education (SRE) for the 21st Century*.[6]

After a short while in the wilderness, PSHE's star has risen again as the need for better mental health support has become an increasing concern for teachers. Issues of consent, risk, safety and sexual harassment have also emerged as key drivers for a new PSHE curriculum. Concerns over radicalisation led to the 'Prevent' duty[7] and the guidance around 'Fundamental British Values'.[8]

In 2017 the government announced that Relationship Education – there is still some consternation about why 'Sex' has been removed from the title – will be made statutory in primary schools, while RSE will be made statutory in secondary schools.

Part of PSHE's problem has always been that, despite the positive messages from all political parties and from Ofsted, it has never been afforded the statutory status that would ensure its part in the overall school curriculum. PSHE is the forgotten subject, quickly displaced by fire-alarm practice, assemblies and open days, its place in teaching time eaten up by spelling tests, extra reading and the other many pressures of a busy timetable.

Even so, PSHE is surely the backbone of all schools. If pupils are to negotiate and thrive in a fast, technology-driven world, then they need to gain the knowledge, understanding and above all skills to do

5 Department for Education and Employment (DfEE) (2000) *Sex and Relationships Education Guidance.* London: DfEE.

6 Brook, PSHE Association and Sex Education Forum (2014) *Sex and Relationships Education (SRE) for the 21st Century.* London: Brook, PSHE Association and Sex Education Forum.

7 Department for Education (DfE) (2015) *Protecting Children from Radicalisation.* London: DfE.

8 Department for Education (DfE) (2014) *Promoting Fundamental British Values as Part of SMSC in Schools.* London: DfE.

this. As educators we have a responsibility to ensure that the pupils in our care are equipped for this world, just as we have a duty of care to ensure that they are numerate and literate. And teaching and learning in PSHE must be at the same standard, and taught with the same dedication and attention to detail, as every other subject. It is the bedrock on which learning takes place.

The PSHE Association says this best in the introduction to its *Programme of Study* (2017):[9] 'As part of a whole-school approach, PSHE education develops the qualities and attributes pupils need to thrive as individuals, family members and members of society.' It also states that: 'PSHE education can help schools to reduce or remove many of the barriers to learning experienced by pupils, significantly improving their capacity to learn and achieve.'

✱ SOMETHING TO THINK ABOUT

For more information about PSHE, the following publications and guidance may be of interest:

- PSHE Association (2017) *Programme of Study*. London: PSHE Association.

- Brook, PSHE Association and Sex Education Forum (2014) *Sex and Relationships Education (SRE) for the 21st Century*. London: Brook, PSHE Association and Sex Education Forum.

- Macdonald, Sir A. (2009) *Independent Review of the Proposal to Make Personal, Social, Health and Economic (PSHE) Education Statutory*. London: Department for Children, Schools and Families.

- Chief Secretary to the Treasury (2003) *Every Child Matters*. London: The Stationery Office.

- Department for Education and Skills (2005) *Social and Emotional Aspects of Learning: Improving Behaviour, Improving Learning*. London: Department for Education and Skills.

---

9   PSHE Association (2017) *Programme of Study.* London: PSHE Association.

- Department of Health and Department for Education and Skills (2005) *National Healthy Schools Programme.* London: Department of Health and Department for Education and Skills.

Getting to grips with guidance

Given this rather chequered past, how do we know what is *law*, what is *guidance* and what is considered *good practice* in PSHE?

While PSHE is not currently a National Curriculum subject area, the National Curriculum guidance[10] states that 'all schools should make provision for Personal, Social, Health and Economic Education (PSHE), drawing on good practice. Schools are also free to include other subjects or topics of their choice in planning and designing their own programme of education.' In other words, PSHE is valued as a delivery vehicle for teaching key skills, and while there is an expectation that schools will teach PSHE, they are free to choose what, where and how they teach it.

The Department for Education (DfE) goes even further in its encouragement of PSHE in its PSHE Education Guidance advice (2014),[11] saying that, 'while we believe that it is for schools to tailor their local PSHE programme to reflect the needs of their pupils, we expect schools to use their PSHE education programme to equip pupils with a sound understanding of risk and with the knowledge and skills necessary to make safe and informed decisions.'

In terms of further content coverage, the same document adds that: 'Schools should seek to use PSHE education to build, where appropriate, on the statutory content already outlined in the National Curriculum, the basic school curriculum and in statutory guidance on: drug education, financial education, sex and relationship education (SRE) and the importance of physical activity and diet for a healthy lifestyle.' So we do have some guidance about the sort of areas that PSHE should seek to address.

And in the Children and Social Work Bill 2017, 'Relationships and Sex Education' is to be statutory from 2019. The change from

---

10 Department for Education (DfE) (2014) *The National Curriculum in Primary School.* London: DfE.

11 PSHE Association (2017) *Programme of Study.* London: PSHE Association.

'Sex and Relationship Education' (SRE) in placing the 'R' first indicates the DfE's commitment to developing positive relationships as well as teaching the biological aspects. 'All primary schools (maintained, academies or independent) will be required to provide relationships education (and will retain their current choice to teach age-appropriate sex education).' It seems likely that PSHE itself will also be made statutory, and indeed this change would make sense.

In order to build on the excellent practice already developed in schools, this is a good time to review planning and provision in PSHE teaching and learning and to make sure it's the best it can be. The PSHE Association is a key partner in this development. While it's essential that every school builds its PSHE curriculum around the needs of the pupils in that school, there are principles that give a solid grounding in good practice and should always be followed. The PSHE Association has compiled 'Ten Principles of PSHE Education', which you'll find in the Appendix. It's worth making sure that you keep these to hand and refer to them on a regular basis when planning and teaching lessons.

Researching effectiveness

Teaching PSHE is all very well, but if the subject isn't part of the National Curriculum and there's no test in it, how do we know whether the teaching actually works?

It has always been tricky to demonstrate the links between wellbeing and academic attainment, but research is beginning to back up what we already know from experience: that healthier, happier, safer children who are ready to learn make better progress in school. We know, professionally and anecdotally, that primary school is about educating the whole child, but in the pressure-cooker created by government goals and the quest for academic attainment and progress, it's good to know that there are indeed clear links between attainment and wellbeing. Fiona Brooks[12] describes the links in this way: 'The promotion of physical and mental health simultaneously can offer great benefits for children, working dynamically to create

---

12　Brooks, F. (2013) 'Life Stage: School Years.' In S.C. Davies (ed.) *Chief Medical Officer's Annual Report 2012. Our Children Deserve Better: Prevention Pays.* London: Department of Health.

a virtuous circle that keeps reinforcing overall health, wellbeing and achievement.' PSHE plays an important part in creating this virtuous circle.

A study by the University of Hertfordshire reinforces this. The study found clear links between high-quality PSHE lessons, reduced levels of bullying and increased feelings of school belonging.[13] These links match findings from Ofsted's *Not Yet Good Enough* report (2013),[14] in which inspectors noted a close correlation between the inspection grade that schools were awarded for overall effectiveness and that awarded for PSHE teaching and learning. In other words, an outstanding school is aspirational in all areas of school life and learning, and places high-quality PSHE high on the agenda.

A briefing for schools from Public Health England[15] states unequivocally that:

1. pupils with better health and wellbeing are likely to achieve better academically

2. effective social and emotional competencies are associated with greater health and wellbeing, and better achievement

3. the culture, ethos and environment of a school influences the health and wellbeing of pupils and their readiness to learn

4. a positive association exists between academic attainment and physical activity levels of pupils.

There is also research linking happiness and positive mental health to children's attainment (e.g. American psychologist Seligman's work on linking happiness, grit and academic attainment).[16] It's possible to disappear down the rabbit hole of combined research projects about character, grit, determination and a growth mindset. These concepts

---

13 University of Hertfordshire and PSHE Association (2016) *Evidence Briefing: PSHE Education, Pupil Wellbeing and Safety at School.* London: PSHE Association. The study reported associations between PSHE lessons on personal and social skills and feelings of belonging and strong relationships at school.

14 Ofsted (2013) *Not Yet Good Enough: Personal, Social, Health and Economic Education in Schools – Personal Social and Health Education in English Schools in 2012.* London: Ofsted.

15 Public Health England (2014) *The Link Between Pupil Health and Wellbeing and Attainment: A Briefing for Head Teachers, Governors and Staff in Education Settings.* London: Public Health England.

16 Seligman's publications include: Seligman, M. (2012) *Flourish: A Visionary New Understanding of Happiness and Wellbeing.* New York: Free Press.

can seem very current as the media bemoan Generation Z's 'lack of resilience' and the 'snowflake' generation who are more interested in social media than in living in the real world. It's worth being a little cautious with these concepts and ideas, however; rather than committing wholesale to them in school, it is preferable to think about the most effective way of teaching pupils to thrive in the world, both now and in the future.

PSHE can make a significant contribution to the whole-school approach, but the subject needs to be well planned, well taught, well led and well resourced. In the following sections, we'll delve into what this could look like in your school.

❀ SOMETHING TO THINK ABOUT

Think about how you decide what to teach in PSHE in your school. Is it based on carefully planned lessons that match the needs of the pupils in your school or is it based on how you've always done things, what resources you have, or the latest trends? How do you know whether your PSHE teaching and learning works, and how do you link this to academic attainment?

Linking SMSC and PSHE

SMSC development is the glue that holds together many aspects of teaching and learning and education that don't necessarily come under the banner of a class-based subject area. It's inspected by Ofsted and is a requirement of all schools, but it is hard to pin down as it can be abstract. In this section we'll try to unpack what it is, where it fits with PSHE, and how SMSC and PSHE may serve each other.

Go back to that question of what you want for every Year Six pupil leaving your school. Think also about your own school – what is your school's unique selling point (USP)? What are the key factors that distinguish your school from the one down the road? What makes parents want to send their children to your school? Films are summed up with loglines – a sentence or two that captures the story in an appealing way – and it might be worth just thinking about what you might choose as a logline for your own school:

- 'A large urban primary school in a diverse, vibrant community, with a focus on personal learning and creativity.'

- 'A small, family-orientated school with community at its heart.'

- 'A faith school in a semi-rural area which prides itself on sport and academic attainment.'

Every school has the aim of providing an excellent academic education, and mission statements often contain something about pastoral care, but your school ethos may be less easy to define.

SMSC captures some of the elements of your school's logline. It's about the elements of school that you can feel, see and hear. Although SMSC is often hard to quantify, before you start planning your PSHE programme to complement and support it, it's important to define what SMSC is in your school and how you address it. If SMSC is the overarching feel and ethos of school, PSHE is the more tangible way of addressing pupil needs – but how do they fit together?

The Citizenship Foundation breaks SMSC down into its component parts, such as this:[17]

> *Spiritual:* Explore beliefs and experience; respect faiths, feelings and values; enjoy learning about oneself, others and the surrounding world; use imagination and creativity; reflect.

Ofsted's definition of 'spiritual' builds on this:[18]

> Pupils' spiritual development is shown by pupils':

- ability to be reflective about their own beliefs, religious or otherwise, that inform their perspective on life and their interest in and respect for different people's faiths, feelings and values

- sense of enjoyment and fascination in learning about themselves, others and the world around them

- use of imagination and creativity in their learning willingness to reflect on their experiences.

---

17 Quotes from the Citizenship Foundation are from their SMSC website: www. doingsmsc.org.uk.

18 Quotes from Ofsted are from: Ofsted (2015) *School Inspection Handbook.* London: Ofsted.

Citizenship Foundation:

Moral: Recognise right and wrong; respect the law; understand consequences; investigate moral and ethical issues; offer reasoned views.

Ofsted's definition of 'moral':

Pupils' moral development is shown by their:

- ability to recognise the difference between right and wrong and to readily apply this understanding in their own lives, recognise legal boundaries and, in so doing, respect the civil and criminal law of England

- understanding of the consequences of their behaviour and actions

- interest in investigating and offering reasoned views about moral and ethical issues and ability to understand and appreciate the viewpoints of others on these issues.

Citizenship Foundation:

Social: Use a range of social skills; participate in the local community; appreciate diverse viewpoints; participate, volunteer and co-operate; resolve conflict; engage with the 'British Values' of democracy, the rule of law, liberty, respect and tolerance.

Ofsted's definition of 'social':

Pupils' social development is shown by their:

- use of a range of social skills in different contexts, for example working and socialising with other pupils, including those from different religious, ethnic and socio-economic backgrounds

- willingness to participate in a variety of communities and social settings, including by volunteering, cooperating well with others and being able to resolve conflicts effectively

- acceptance and engagement with the fundamental British values of democracy, the rule of law, individual liberty and mutual respect and tolerance of those with different faiths and beliefs; they develop and demonstrate skills and attitudes that will allow them to participate fully in and contribute positively to life in modern Britain.

Citizenship Foundation:

Cultural: Appreciate cultural influences; appreciate the role of Britain's parliamentary system; participate in culture opportunities; understand, accept, respect and celebrate diversity.

Ofsted's definition of cultural:

Pupils' cultural development is shown by their:

- understanding and appreciation of the wide range of cultural influences that have shaped their own heritage and those of others

- understanding and appreciation of the range of different cultures within school and further afield as an essential element of their preparation for life in modern Britain

- knowledge of Britain's democratic parliamentary system and its central role in shaping our history and values, and in continuing to develop Britain

- willingness to participate in and respond positively to artistic, musical, sporting and cultural opportunities

- interest in exploring, improving understanding of and showing respect for different faiths and cultural diversity and the extent to which they understand, accept, respect and celebrate diversity, as shown by their tolerance and attitudes towards different religious, ethnic and socio-economic groups in the local, national and global communities.

If we take the moral element as an example, it's possible to see where PSHE contributes to SMSC, as shown in Table 1.1.

Teaching values is always tricky. Values come primarily from one's family and cultural background, and it's our job as teachers to help pupils develop their own moral framework, to challenge any misconceptions, and to offer support in finding further help. Before teaching values, think about where your *own* values come from — that is, from what happened in your upbringing, from your family circumstances, and from the occurrences that shaped you into the adult you have become. There may be things that you're passionate about and other things that make you upset or angry. Recognising these potential trigger points may help you approach values-based teaching in a more impartial way. It's not our job to impose our own values on pupils, but to help them develop their own within the parameters of school.

Table 1.1 How PSHE can contribute to the 'moral' element of SMSC

SMSC (Citizenship Foundation)	PSHE
'Recognise right and wrong...'	Debating and discussing moral and ethical issues, and having the opportunity to debate issues and scenarios in a safe environment.
'...respect the law...'	Recognising and understanding laws and how they protect us (e.g. online), and having the opportunity to discuss laws, rights and responsibilities.
'...understand consequences...'	Considering the outcomes of various scenarios; considering decision-making; learning about conflict management; and thinking about friendships and other relationships.
'...investigate moral and ethical issues; offer reasoned views.'	Debating various scenarios in a safe environment; considering different viewpoints; being assertive; learning to communicate effectively; and developing healthy relationships and friendships.

Quotes from the Citizenship Foundation (www.doingsmsc.org.uk)

Regardless of our personal values, however, there is guidance in the form of a document from the government, *Promoting Fundamental British Values as Part of SMSC in Schools*.[19] This document sets out requirements for maintained schools in promoting British values through SMSC (and thus via PSHE too, where applicable). Schools need to be able to demonstrate that they are actively promoting these values and 'challenging opinions or behaviours in school that are contrary to Fundamental British Values'.

Ofsted inspectors look for evidence that schools are delivering SMSC and 'British values', so where does PSHE come in? The document states that, through their provision of SMSC, schools should:

---

19 Department for Education (DfE) (2014) *Promoting Fundamental British Values as Part of SMSC in Schools*. London: DfE.

Enable students to develop their self-knowledge, self-esteem and self-confidence.

This is definite PSHE territory. Through the spiral curriculum of well-planned PSHE teaching and learning, with active, engaging sessions, pupils should have plenty of opportunities to discover more about themselves and their own behaviours, to develop their understanding of self, and to develop their self-confidence.

Enable students to distinguish right from wrong and to respect the civil and criminal law of England.

Through PSHE, pupils should have the chance to debate, discuss and evaluate decision-making, while being reminded that laws are there to protect and support them.

Encourage students to accept responsibility for their behaviour, show initiative, and to understand how they can contribute positively to the lives of those living and working in the locality of the school and to society more widely.

PSHE learning should explore behaviour and feelings and should offer pupils opportunities to take responsibility, for example by leading a group, making decisions or talking in public. Through PSHE they should develop empathy and understanding of the lives of others, and come to recognise that we have a responsibility to live as active citizens in our communities. Elements of charity support – local, national and international – can help pupils to develop an understanding of their place in the global society.

Enable students to acquire a broad general knowledge of and respect for public institutions and services in England.

Elements of the PSHE curriculum on democracy, those that help us and the local community, can contribute to this element. Broadening the PSHE curriculum with visits (e.g. to the town hall) and visitors (e.g. a local MP or a police officer) can address this element too.

Further tolerance and harmony between different cultural traditions by enabling students to acquire an appreciation of and respect for their own and other cultures.

Think about building this into your PSHE curriculum, so that all faiths and cultures in your school are valued and supported. How do you celebrate difference and encourage a mutual respect?

Encourage respect for other people.

We use the word 'respect' a lot in PSHE, but it's important to explore exactly what it means and what 'respect' looks like in action. Explore ideas around manners, behaviour, working together, empathy, and asking for support and help when needed. Anti-bullying work should include celebrating difference and similarity.

Encourage respect for democracy and support for participation in the democratic processes, including respect for the basis on which the law is made and applied in England.

Include learning about the democratic process in your PSHE curriculum as part of 'Citizenship'. By exploring the democratic process and by taking part in school-based democratic processes, children will gain a better understanding of how the process works and how we can express ourselves if we feel our voices are not being heard.

It's worth remembering, however, that PSHE is only one part of the larger picture of delivering SMSC across the school, so PSHE needs to be mapped carefully to address any needs or gaps. A thoughtful curriculum is tailored to the needs of the pupils in your school, and that means that you must know what their needs are. How do you identify these? By looking at data about the make-up of pupils, and their academic and pastoral needs; and by drilling down into those data and creating plans to address gaps in learning and making any necessary improvements. Examples include whole-school targets such as raising standards in writing across Key Stage 2, ensuring well-planned assessment in all subject areas, or meeting the needs of specific groups, such as making sure that young carers can access pastoral support or that pupils who have free school meals are given opportunities to access extra-curricular activities. By giving PSHE high status in school, leaders demonstrate its value within the school community.

❋ SOMETHING TO THINK ABOUT

The Citizenship Foundation has developed an SMSC Quality Mark, which can help schools to monitor, evaluate and celebrate their SMSC provision. The Quality Mark can act as a key piece of evidence that your school is fulfilling the SMSC requirements.

For more information, take a look at the National SMSC Quality Mark website: www.smscqualitymark.org.uk.

Approaching difference and diversity in PSHE

The Equality Act 2010 introduced a duty of care that applies to all public-sector bodies, including maintained schools and academies, which includes 'protected characteristics' such as race, disability, sex, age, religion or belief, sexual orientation, pregnancy, maternity, and gender reassignment. In addition, public bodies must have due regard[20] to the need to:

- eliminate discrimination and other conduct that is prohibited by the Act; advance equality of opportunity between people who share a protected characteristic and people who do not share it

- foster good relations across all characteristics – between people who share a protected characteristic and people who do not share it.

In deciding whether to make an 'outstanding' judgement in relation to teaching and learning, Ofsted[21] will look for evidence that:

teachers are quick to challenge stereotypes and the use of derogatory language in lessons and around the school. Resources and teaching strategies reflect and value the diversity of pupils' experiences and provide pupils with a comprehensive understanding of people and communities beyond their immediate experience.

Not only are schools expected to *ensure* equality of opportunity, but they must also *advance* equality of opportunity and *foster good relations*, and this is where PSHE comes in. PSHE can provide a forum where issues relating to difference and diversity are addressed, challenged and explored.

---

20 Department for Education (DfE) (2014) *The Equality Act 2010 and Schools: Departmental Advice for School Leaders, School Staff, Governing Bodies and Local Authorities.* London: DfE.

21 Ofsted (2015) *School Inspection Handbook.* London: Ofsted.

Tackling diversity in PSHE may seem like a tricky topic, but if we are to ensure that pupils live and thrive in a modern multicultural society, then we need to be talking to children about issues of diversity from a young age. Children will be very aware of current issues of living together in a complex and challenging society – Brexit, the refugee crisis, conflicting messages in the media, personal experiences and incidents of discrimination – and we need to ensure that diversity is more than an annual international evening and a message that 'Everyone is equal'.

Gender stereotyping and attitudes to gender offer a good place to start. No matter how even-handed we think we may be, there will probably be some aspects of gender difference that need addressing in school. Exploring these in the safe environment of PSHE will encourage discussion and empathy. As always with PSHE, it's not about lecturing or berating pupils but encouraging them to think and challenging any preconceived ideas. Look at pictures of toys, for example, and talk about whether they are 'boy' toys or 'girl' toys, and how we know. Is it okay for girls to play with construction toys and cars and for boys to play with dolls or dressing-up clothes? Encourage children to think about where the messages come from, and whether they are rules or suggestions. Talk about sports and careers. Can girls and women be scientists, mechanics and footballers? Can boys and men be nurses, dancers and stay-at-home parents? Consider the language we use with boys and girls, and whether there are differences. Explore phrases like 'man up' or 'run like a girl', and explicit and implicit expectations of behaviour 'appropriate' to particular sexes, such as boys not being expected to show their feelings or to talk about them and girls being 'mean' or 'catty'.

Ensure that all staff use phrases such as 'I need some children to help carry those benches' rather than 'I need some strong boys to help carry the benches'. Do you use gender-neutral occupation words like 'police officer' and 'firefighter'? This is not simply an exercise in political correctness, but a reflection on the world these children are entering. At the time of writing, the leader of the country is a woman, as is the head of the Metropolitan Police and the head of the London Fire Brigade. There are other key women leaders across the country and the world, and the way we talk needs to reflect that.

In PSHE lessons, make sure that both boys and girls take turns in leading groups or activities. Teach both to use a wide emotional vocabulary, to recognise feelings that are good and not so good, and to express themselves effectively. Actively teach children the difference between aggressive, passive and assertive behaviours and language, so that they can use these in creating better communication both offline and online.

● CASE STUDY

I wanted to talk about gender stereotyping with my Year One class so I split them into two mixed groups, one with me and one with the teaching assistant. The adults read the following to each group and asked them to help fill in the gaps: 'Sam is six years old like you in Year One. Sam likes to play... at school Sam's favourite subject is... and at play time Sam likes to play... Sam's favourite colour is... and Sam's favourite toy is... When Sam is grown up Sam wants to be a...' At the end of one story was 'Sam is a girl', and at the end of the other 'Sam is a boy'. We then let the two groups discuss and agree on answers. As a whole class we compared answers and discussed them. Even at this young age the group gave female Sam the colour pink, drawing, skipping and being a teacher. Male Sam liked red, football, Maths and wanted to be a builder. This acted as a starting point to discuss whether female Sam might like playing football and if male Sam could enjoy skipping. The lesson wasn't about changing children's minds or saying they couldn't play football or like pink but was about opening their eyes to a broader way of thinking. Perhaps one of those children would go on to feel a bit more confident if they wanted to try something new.

Year One teacher

With older children, gender stereotyping and attitudes to gender can be considered in relation to media messages and the question of whether we have to act or look a certain way because messages in the media tell us we should. Talk about the need to recognise that there are different points of view, and that seeing something or reading something in the media doesn't mean we have to look like that or act in that way. Through scenarios and discussions, teach skills around being assertive and managing peer pressure, so that if they are faced with a situation in which they experience direct or indirect discrimination, children will have a toolkit of techniques to deal with this and can ask for help if needed.

Racial, cultural or religious stereotyping is also a key topic for PSHE. We might assume that everything is okay if there are few overt incidents of racism and if everyone seems to be getting on with one another, but exploring deeper issues can be part of PSHE, whether or not your school has a multicultural mix. Acknowledge the differences as well as the similarities and be sure to address any misconceptions or misunderstandings between groups of pupils. Invite faith leaders, community leaders and family members to talk about their lifestyles. Celebrate differences in language, family life and culture, and encourage respect between all groups. If your school is not very mixed, then make a connection with a multicultural school and learn about each other. Use video-chatting to see and talk to one another and exchange learning opportunities. Ensure that learning is protected by robust methods of reporting and dealing with discrimination so that pupils feel valued and listened to and any problems are ironed out quickly.

Allana Gay (a deputy head and founder of BAMEed, which offers a forum for Black, Asian and Minority Ethnic (BAME) school leaders) believes that PSHE is one of the contexts in which we can be open about discussing our differences. I asked Allana Gay for her thoughts:

> We are all not equal so let's stop saying we are. Think of equality as an aspiration of treatment rather than a state of being. In the former sense we are open to acknowledging the current status quo, examining why change is necessary (or not!) and empowering our students to carry this aspiration forward. The other gives a false understanding of societal structures and processes that allow some to flourish faster and seemingly easier than others. PSHE is the subject that 'prepares students for life and work in modern Britain'. Is it not obligatory on educators to discuss why social class, economic wealth and ethnicity are powerful precursors to future prospects within Britain? If we cannot find a way to facilitate this discussion and build on ideas then it will never be normal.
>
> I do not speak of a victim/blame discussion that engenders resentment between groups but a recognition that features of our birth initialises out societal encounters. In this way students and educators will bring recognition of PSHE as a foundation of citizenship and citizenship as key to the evolution of British society.

We are not equal, but through our work in schools we can keep working towards that goal of equity.

Allana Gay

In the same way that Allana Gay talks about facilitating and normalising discussion on difference and diversity, Shaun Dellenty (also a deputy head, and founder of an education charity, Inclusion for All) believes that openness is key. As an openly gay man who experienced bullying at school, he is keen that we shouldn't shy away from talking about same-sex relationships and families with same-sex parents. As recently as 1988, schools were not allowed to 'promote the teaching in any maintained school of the acceptability of homosexuality as a pretended family relationship', but section 28 of the Local Government Act 1988[22] was quickly repealed in 2000. With equal-marriage legislation in force from 2013 in England, Scotland and Wales, schools now have a responsibility to normalise a range of relationships and families. Even so, talking about same-sex relationships and using the language associated with them can still feel tricky for some.

Shaun Dellenty has this advice from his own experiences:

In 2009 in my London primary school we discovered (via pupil voice) that 75% of children were hearing 'gay' being used on a daily negative basis in school, from peers but also sometimes from staff members and parents. In 2009 the use of 'That's so gay' to describe something as uncool, unwanted or without worth was endemic across the UK.

That the word 'gay' even developed an additional use as a pejorative term is worthy of a chapter in itself; however, suffice to say that as a middle-aged gay man myself, cultural adaptation of the word gay to describe the 'lowest common denominator' represented the latest lineage in pejorative language used in schools to describe LGBT+ (Lesbian Gay Bisexual Transgender Plus[23]) people, incorporating such offensive terms as 'faggot', 'bender', 'batty boy' and 'queer'. This latest iteration attempted to sully the term that some gay human beings had identified with in order to reframe their lives more positively in a prejudicial world into something more joyful. I would hear 'That's so gay' on the

---

22 Local Government Act 1988: www.legislation.gov.uk.
23 The plus in 'LGBT+' is to include the spectrum of gender and sexuality.

bus from work, making me wince internally and ponder how my fellow passengers might react if the expression was changed to 'That's so disabled' or 'That's so black'.

In any primary school there will already be a number of children who (perhaps covertly) know they may be emergent LGBT+ (or may have LGBT+ friends and family); 'gay' used in this way is inappropriate as it has the potential to cause emotional harm and enable shame. Simply ordering the whole school community not to use the word 'gay' would have also been inappropriate.

In response I planned assemblies and lessons (using LGBT+ role models as a stimulus) and teachers applied their existing knowledge of teaching *word use* to this specific issue. Teachers taught children the original use of the word 'gay' using examples of age-appropriate poems and stories in which 'gay' meant 'joyful' or 'happy'. Children then wrote and explored using 'gay' in this manner, normalising and ensuring that teaching staff/pupils were able to verbalise the word out loud without any sense of shame or embarrassment. The giggles that had sometimes accompanied classroom use of 'gay' began to dissipate.

Teachers then explored the adaptation of 'gay' to describe homosexual humans, looking at how and why this might have happened, incorporating this work into PSHE, P4C (Philosophy for Children) and assemblies. This opening up of discourse enabled some young people with emergent LGBT+ identities or with LGBT+ friends and families to talk about this with school staff for the very first time, enabling us to further meet their needs.

LGBT+ speakers were invited in to talk in assemblies about what being gay meant to them and how the pejorative use of the term had the potential to add to their sense of 'otherness' or shame. As a follow up, children were invited to explore how and why they were using 'gay' in the playground and at home and the possible negative consequences of this on others. Children themselves came to the conclusion that using 'gay' in a negative context to insult before claiming when caught out that one was 'not meaning to be homophobic' was usually an attempt to avoid sanction and were able to reach the conclusion that use of language can hurt others and comes with responsibility. Children generated word lists of other 'off limits' language and terms that might cause offence or hurt, even if they had not meant to; terms like 'mental' or 'four eyes'.

From these rich discussions arose student-led poster campaigns, role-play class assemblies, podcasts and new school/class rules intended to make clear to *all* stakeholders (including adult visitors to the school) that 'gay' used pejoratively had the same potential to cause harm as the 'n' word to black children if used freely. The relationship of intent to harm and the receiving of pejorative language by a victim was explicitly related to hate crime law which places in high regard the perceptions of the person adversely affected in making a judgement as to whether a crime has occurred.

Students were keen that, once teaching and learning had taken place, should the word 'gay' be used as a curse the perpetrator should be disciplined as would the perpetrator of a racist term. These high-profile campaigns and teaching and learning, sustained over a year and revisited annually during anti-bullying week, resulted in a significant reduction in the use of *all* forms of prejudicial language. Work was shared on social media attracting national interest and triggering many related projects.

One day in late 2010 I met a Year 6 new arrival at the end of playtime. I asked his 'New Arrival Playground Buddy' how he had been getting on.

'He was doing okay,' said the Buddy, 'but then someone missed a goal and he said it was so gay.'

'What did you do?' I asked.

'I told him that in this school we only use the word gay to mean something joyful or happy or to describe someone who is gay – like you Shaun.'

With that I walked away, wiped my eyes and went back to my desk to await the next new pejorative phrase to emerge from the ether.

Shaun Dellenty

The important message from both Allana Gay and Shaun Dellenty is that fostering an atmosphere in which pupils can talk about the issues affecting them, and in which they can be challenged about preconceived ideas and use of language, can lead to the whole school community taking a more positive approach. As Allana Gay states, 'We can keep working towards that goal of equity.'

❋ SOMETHING TO THINK ABOUT

Make sure there are opportunities throughout your PSHE programme to explore ideas about difference and diversity. Make sure also that resources, photographs and film clips reflect a broad society. Picture books, stories and poetry (including spoken-word poetry) can provide good starting points for discussions, so make sure the ones you choose reflect a wide range of characters and families.

When talking about words that hurt, don't shy away from words like 'gay' or 'retarded' or pejorative gender-based language: instead, use these as a starting point to encourage children to think about better words that they could use. In using or writing scenarios for use in PSHE activities, be sure to have a range of characters and family situations, so that thinking and talking about different families becomes part of the norm at school.

See the following for more information:

- *Women's Aid:* This federation has produced an 'Expect Respect Toolkit': www.womensaid.org.uk/what-we-do/safer-futures/expect-respect-educational-toolkit.

- *Dove:* This company runs 'Real' beauty and self-esteem campaigns: www.dove.com/uk/stories/campaigns.html.

- *Pink Stinks:* A campaign that provides information on media stereotyping: www.pinkstinks.co.uk.

- *Let Toys be Toys:* This website has a wide range of resources and links: http://lettoysbetoys.org.uk.

- *Inclusion for All:* Shaun Dellenty's education charity has a wide range of helpful resources, advice and videos. You can also book him to speak at conferences or events: www.inclusionforall.co.uk.

- *Diversity Role Models:* This charity runs workshops and training in schools about homophobic bullying: www.diversityrolemodels.org.

- *BAMEed:* You can follow #BAMEed on Twitter for discussions about being a BAME school leader and find links to resources and training opportunities.

Thinking about values

Many aspects of PSHE can be really personal, so before you embark on teaching PSHE it's a good idea to reflect on where your own values, attitudes and ideas come from. We are all the unique products of our personal experiences of parenting, schooling, culture, class, race and faith, and the thousands of incidents and experiences that make up our lives.

Our values touch on every aspect of teaching. They inform how we teach and the *passion* with which we teach. In general, it's important to remain neutral and balanced in your teaching – to give information, to encourage, to discuss and sometimes to challenge. It is not our job to persuade children to a particular point of view, except when an issue arises in relation to safeguarding. While your own views may differ from those of your pupils, they should not determine your approach to teaching.

Be aware, however, that some issues raised in PSHE may touch a nerve or raise unresolved issues from your own life. Be conscious of these and be prepared to deal with any problems that arise. If you yourself experienced being bullied, for example, then bullying might be a sensitive topic. In that case, if a child expresses strong views about bullying or if a bullying incident emerges in a lesson, then your own response may be rooted in your personal experiences. Similarly, if you hold a strong view on an issue that may clash with a view from another culture or faith, then you may need to remind yourself that your role is not to impose your own views but to encourage pupils to see all sides of the argument.

❋ SOMETHING TO THINK ABOUT

Read through the following questions about teaching and think about your responses to them in relation to PSHE. Jot down notes if you think they would be useful, and consider where you could access help if you need further support. With your responses in mind, consider any changes or adaptations you need to make to your PSHE teaching.

The Education Support Partnership offers a wealth of information about teachers' mental health and how to access support. See www.educationsupportpartnership.org.uk.

- *Why teaching?* Maybe on a Monday afternoon, when the week has barely started and you've had a nightmare of a day, you may be asking this in earnest! We were each drawn into teaching for a reason, however, and it's good to remind yourself why you took this route. Strip away the practicalities and get to the heart of *why* – it might be because you had a good education yourself and wanted to replicate that for other children, or because you had an indifferent or difficult education and you didn't want others to experience the same, or because you wanted to work with children, or to make a difference. Whatever your own reason for becoming a teacher, how does this 'why' impact on your PSHE teaching? Do you teach *as* passionately or *less* passionately in PSHE? Why? How can you bring that original love for teaching into PSHE?

- *What do you absolutely love about teaching?* That moment when a child gets a concept that was difficult for them? The moments when you're a team who are succeeding and having fun? Bringing your own style into the classroom? Transforming dry learning objectives into vibrant learning experiences? That moment when every child is on task and engaged? Whatever it is that you love, how can you ensure that those moments happen in your PSHE lessons too? And if they're *not* happening, why not? How can you make changes to ensure that there are more of these moments?

- *What in teaching makes you despair?* (The other side of the same coin.) When behaviour management fails? Worrying about the marking and paperwork that comes after lessons have finished? Whatever it is that makes you despair, is there anything you can do to ensure that PSHE doesn't fall into this category? Are there other behaviour-management techniques that might help, for example, asking for the support of additional adults? How could you make sure that any marking, assessment and paperwork is meaningful and helpful rather than an additional burden?

- *What aspects of PSHE do you embrace?* Perhaps it's the experience that the atmosphere is different in PSHE lessons, or the opportunity to get stuck into some challenging topics, or the breakthrough moments, or the challenge. Whatever it is that you enjoy, can you put more of that into your lessons? Can you share your expertise and enthusiasm with other colleagues who may struggle with the same aspects?

- *What aspects of PSHE do you find a real challenge?* If there are tricky topics that make you anxious because of previous experiences, how could you access support with these? What do you need to do yourself to help overcome your worries? Would more detailed planning help, or could you practise using new terminology or vocabulary until it feels normal? Ask your PSHE subject leader for help; plan together with a colleague from a parallel class, even if you're planning your own in a one form entry school (i.e. in a school with a single entry form each year) and try out one new idea before embarking on a whole lesson.

- *What unique skills do you bring to PSHE?* Bring your own flavour to PSHE, whether it's a passion for music, sport, IT or drama, or for collaborative or immersive learning. Don't be afraid to bring your own style to PSHE or your pupils will experience these lessons as 'different'. PSHE needs to be taught like any other subject – use your unique teaching style and personality.

- *What makes you...you?* Think about your personal philosophy. If you were a brand and had a strapline (like a candidate on *The Apprentice*, but without the cheesy bombast!), what might it be? How can you bring individuality and uniqueness to your PSHE lessons that will help transform them from words on a plan into the best version of your teaching self?

- *Where can you go for help and support?* Colleagues, continuing professional development (CPD), books, journals and periodicals? If a deeper-rooted problem has emerged, consider whether you need to talk to a professional or need more time to reflect and talk.

Chapter Two

PLANNING YOUR SCHOOL'S PSHE PROGRAMME

Now we've looked at the broader picture of PSHE and placed it in context, it's time to consider how to build an outstanding curriculum in your school. This chapter deals with where PSHE sits in the curriculum, how to fit it into an already busy timetable, and how to make sure it dovetails neatly with other curriculum areas so that it is seen as meaningful and reflects your school's teaching and learning rather than simply being a bolt-on activity. Embedding PSHE firmly into your school's very fabric will ensure that learning feels joined up and that there's a spread of support across the whole school community.

Building a spiral curriculum

One of the reasons that PSHE as a subject may not have the impact it could or should is if it looks like a Jenga tower rather than a spiral. As anyone knows who has played the wobbly wooden-block game, if you overload the top you get gaps at the bottom, and if there are crucial parts missing then eventually the whole structure collapses. Much better to build a curriculum on solid foundations and climbing upwards like a spiral staircase, with each step carrying you upwards while also allowing you to see what has gone before and what is still to come.

With a well-planned spiral curriculum the stronger foundations allow for better teaching and learning and greater impact. A good example of where the Jenga model may often be found is in RSE. RSE is quite often taught in upper Key Stage 2, arriving out of nowhere and being started on top of a rather wobbly foundation. The whispers may go around the Year Six pupils, and parents may start to panic and stockpile books about puberty. Everyone may become a bit anxious and there may be an air of waiting for the whole thing to collapse – teachers worrying about teaching it wrong, pupils worried about what it's all about, and parents not sure how to help their children.

With a spiral curriculum, children start up the staircase in the Foundation Stage, with age-appropriate learning. Each year thereafter pupils revisit the PSHE topics and recap and consolidate their learning, so that each year they move on, step by step. With that approach, you can ensure that pupils are introduced to a range of topics and have the time and opportunity to explore and develop their knowledge, skills and understanding around the topic.

As a comparison, flinging a couple of RSE lessons into upper KS2 – lessons that are all 'S' and not much 'R' – is a bit like starting by teaching Astrophysics to a class who may not even know the basics. Some children will have heard of sex and will try to keep up; some might have watched a television programme about it or talked to their parents about it; and many will be a bit flummoxed and out of their depth… and yet this is how many PSHE topics are taught. Let's go back to RSE and see how a spiral curriculum might work.

RSE in the Early Years is concerned with learning about all sorts of relationships, interacting with peers and adults, and keeping ourselves safe and healthy. That message is repeated in Year One with some added work on 'My Body', changes from baby to toddler to five years old, and further skills in developing relationships with a wider range of people. In Year Two the children recap on how we change, and also learn about hygiene and keeping clean, healthy and safe, and about managing simple risks. By Year Three, relationships, including friendships, begin to get more complex and there is some further work on bullying, on conflict resolution and on people who help us when we have problems or concerns, and some thinking about growing up. By Year Four you might begin to explore in very simple terms the body changes that happen in puberty and the fact that children are growing up both emotionally and physically. This leads into Year Five, which includes further work on puberty and beginning to learn about adult relationships and consent. By Year Six, you can recap on puberty, on the changing nature of relationships and on growing up, plus safety, hygiene and the biological aspects of sex and conception. You've built your spiral curriculum!

The list above is a suggestion only, as you will know your pupils and their needs best; but it helps if you plan a spiral curriculum that grows along with the children, and having that curriculum in place gives a sense of security. Now imagine that every parent who sends their child to your school knows about this curriculum and is just as aware of PSHE topics as they are of which spellings are being covered. Across the board, the stress levels begin to go down as the carefully planned lessons create real impact. We'll cover RSE further later, as it's one of those tricky topics, but let's think now about other key PSHE topics that can be built into a spiral curriculum.

- *Drug and alcohol education:* This starts in the Early Years with simple hygiene and health messages, and builds throughout the years until upper Key Stage 2 when pupils acquire knowledge about drugs and alcohol, develop skills in managing risk around them, and explore social norms as well as laws.

- *Anti-bullying:* This starts with learning about relationships and communicating with others, the definition of 'bullying' (as opposed to simply falling out with your friends), and growing into more complex ways of managing conflict, asking for help and developing skills of empathy. Do the children have enough opportunities to practise their communication and empathy skills so that they can recognise and report bullying?

- *Healthy lifestyles:* Again, for a truly spiral curriculum, beware of covering the same topics year in, year out. Are pupils really developing and building on skills in making choices and managing their own health? Is your curriculum just about eating 'five a day' or do pupils have a chance to practise skills in reading food labels, to learn about the sugar in drinks, to plan and make simple recipes and to explore a range of physical activities, building on skills as they develop?

These are just a few examples of where PSHE topics can be patchy and wobbly like the Jenga tower or just go around in circles until everyone (especially the teacher!) is bored of saying or hearing the same things year after year.

❊ SOMETHING TO THINK ABOUT

Take one PSHE-related topic from your school's scheme of work and trace it from the Early Years to the end of Year Six (or the top of your school). Does the planning allow you to revisit and build on new skills each year? If not, what tweaks and changes could be made so that it becomes a spiral with strong foundations?

Understanding what children need

The world changes so fast that it can make your head spin. Think back to this time last year. What events have changed the world since then? What has happened locally? How did social media react? What inventions, memes and language have come into daily use? Much can happen even in a single year, and if we start thinking back 5, 10 or 20 years, we will see that the world has undergone vast changes.

So what does this mean for the pupils in our care? They are growing up in a world of complex technology and they are digital natives. They are surrounded by the constant chatter of the online world and need vital skills to survive and thrive in that world.

Try this activity with your colleagues. Take a sheet of paper and divide it into two. On one side, jot down memories of things you experienced when you were a primary-age child – how and where you accessed television and entertainment, what books you read and how you read them, what you were aware of in the wider world, what activities you did outside of school, and what you did at school. Then, on the other side, jot down the equivalent things that children in your school experience today and look at the differences.

What skills might they need to develop in order to thrive in this changing world? Are we still locked into teaching that belongs to our era rather than theirs? Children will understand the concept of social media as an effective means of communication and will experience its influence from a young age, even if they are not yet using it themselves. Social media provide an amazing way of staying in touch and of sharing ideas, views and news and learning about the world, but clearly there are negative aspects too. At some point most of us who use social media will experience trolling, cyber-bullying, or at least others whose beliefs are in direct contrast to our own. And unkind words can come directly into our handheld devices, into our homes and private spaces. It's therefore important that in teaching pupils how to communicate we cover online communication too. While we don't need to teach pupils the ins and outs of Twitter and Snapchat in PSHE – these platforms will probably have been superseded or have changed beyond recognition by the time these pupils are older – we do need to teach them how to behave online. When they are found out (and in some cases prosecuted), online trolls often have little grasp of the impact of their nasty comments and threats. It's easy to be vicious anonymously when there is little chance of being found out, so children need to learn about the power of words and that online communication can be as hurtful as – if not *more* hurtful than – verbal threats. So the skills around behaviour online need to be taught alongside behaviour and managing conflict in real life. Weave these into your PSHE curriculum and help your children to manage their online lives in the future. It's also imperative, of course, that children learn about staying safe online, just as they need to manage their personal safety in the real world. While this is an important part of the computing curriculum, it also needs to be reiterated as part of PSHE teaching and learning.

Advertising used to be mainly limited to print and television, but it now pops up everywhere online. Clever algorithms ensure that adverts are targeted at us and pop up as a constant reminder about how the advertisers think we should live, act and look. If you've just announced your marriage on social media, you'll pretty soon start seeing ads for pregnancy tests and baby products; and as you reach the age of 40 you may see ads about wrinkles and diets. As an adult you may be able simply to ignore these advertisements, but for children the constant reminders can be influential. Think about the continual toy adverts on television between kids' shows. They're loud, colourful and dynamic, and before you know it a new and expensive toy has become a sold-out must-have.

We've also had an explosion in 'fake news' so we need to make sure that children don't unquestionably accept everything they read or see online. Help them to develop critical thinking skills so that they can take a balanced view and make up their own minds.

Of course, this explosion in technology and the pressures that result from constantly being bombarded by messages from advertisers and social media means that mental health issues are on the rise among children and young people,[1] so it's essential that we support pupils in managing and supporting their mental health. Teaching skills around conflict management, resilience and managing feelings will go a long way to helping pupils develop positive mental health. In your PSHE curriculum, make sure that pupils have access to the skills they need to develop and that they can practise these in the safe atmosphere of the classroom. In the high-pressure world of testing and exams, children can be afraid of failure, too, so they need reassurance that it's okay to fail sometimes – it's how we deal with that failure that matters.

Ensure also that there is support for those who need it. If you're planning a lesson that may open up some vulnerabilities, make sure the pupils know where to go for follow-up support if they need it. You might have someone else in school to provide this, such as a counsellor or support teacher; if not, make sure you are available after lessons to talk to pupils. Remind them that they can talk to you or another adult in school and that you will support them with their problems, but explain that you can't offer total confidentiality. Make sure there are leaflets and information for local support services available to families and publicise the free Childline number (0800 1111).

Creating a policy

In order for PSHE to be fully embedded into the whole-school curriculum, it needs to be set within the framework of a strong policy. You'll probably have one lurking on the school system somewhere, but it's important to check that it reflects what you actually do in PSHE teaching and learning and that it also reflects the aims of the school. If you were new to the school as a member of staff, trainee, parent or governor, would you understand exactly how the school intends to teach PSHE and why? Would you be able to see evidence of this policy in action in class?

The policy should start by stating the *overarching aim*: what do you want to achieve for the pupils in your school? One activity that might be worth doing is to get teaching and non-teaching staff members to discuss what they think a pupil leaving your school should have in their

---

1   One in three Childline counselling sessions are related to mental and emotional health and wellbeing issues, including self-harm and suicidal thoughts. NSPCC (2017) *Childline Annual Review 2016/17. Not Alone Anymore: What Children and Young People are Talking to Childline About.* London: NSPCC.

toolkit for life (the first task in this book). What qualities should they have? How will they be equipped so that they can adapt and thrive in the next phase of their life? What do people say when they meet pupils from your school who are out in public? Do people in general know what to expect? The outcomes of this activity could form the basis of your overarching aim for your PSHE programme. Remember your school's USP? How is that reflected in your aim?

Next come *the objectives* that describe how you're going to achieve that aim. Have a look at the PSHE Association's 'Ten Principles of PSHE Education' (in the Appendix) and use those as a starting point for a staff discussion.

Most schools have an in-house style for policies, but you may want to include the following key information:

- *Cover sheet.* Say who the policy was written by, the date when it was ratified by the governing body, the date when it will be reviewed, and where parents and carers can access the policy.

- *Brief introduction.* Set your school in context and add in any key information about the health context.

- *Aim.* Provide an overarching vision for the teaching and learning of PSHE in your school.

- *Objectives.* State a few meaningful objectives for your programme, in plain English.

- *Teaching and learning.* Say how, when and where you teach PSHE. You could include a simple curriculum map or diagram, or links to where readers might find one.

- *Resources.* Say where, when and how resources will be used and where to find them in school. Refer to any schemes that will be followed.

- *Assessment.* Say how, when, why and what you will assess.

- *Equality statement.* Say how you plan to ensure equality as stated in the school's equality statement.

- *Confidentiality.* (Essential for a PSHE policy.) Link your policy with the school's child protection or safeguarding policy.

- *Setting ground rules.* Give brief information on setting ground rules and about the importance of ground rules in PSHE teaching.

- *Visitors in PSHE.* Link to your school's visitor policy or give a brief overview of the key information about engaging visitors in PSHE.

- *Cross-curricular and extra-curricular information.* Note where to find additional mapping of PSHE learning opportunities across the curriculum and how these are supported by extra-curricular activities.

- *Links to other relevant policies.* Such policies may relate to RSE, drugs and alcohol, health and safety, child protection and safeguarding, and equality.

- *Signposting to help.* Say where, when and how children and families may access relevant support in and out of school.

- *PSHE co-ordinator.* Say where and how to access the co-ordinator's support.

Consulting on your school's PSHE policy

It's essential that your PSHE policy is well thought out and reflects the unique needs of your school. While it's tempting to download a template and slot in your own school's details, a policy needs to be a useful working document rather than just another document to show Ofsted.

Make sure there is some time in staff meetings or Inset when you can talk about the PSHE vision for your whole school. One of the complaints levelled against PSHE is that it can be less well regarded than other subjects; it may also be the case that if teachers don't have ownership of the subject they may not teach it as well. PSHE lessons can become an exercise in grabbing a lesson-plan outline designed by someone else and delivering the lesson as quickly as possible before getting back onto solid ground with a more familiar subject area.

Staff who understand the importance of teaching and learning in PSHE have a better understanding of the context. With meaningful lessons, the PSHE teaching and learning becomes more meaningful and relevant too. While the staff training and Inset calendars are likely to be booked to make use of every last second, it's important to spare some time for PSHE too. Simple exercises and activities that invite staff to reflect on why PSHE is important and what high-quality PSHE should look like are a good starting point. Link this to the PSHE objectives so that staff can fully understand the context of the teaching. Enthuse staff by encouraging them to think of the wider context of PSHE teaching and learning and how this contributes to raising standards.

Make sure that all staff have an opportunity to read and review the PSHE policy in draft form. If it's not possible for all staff members to read the policy and give feedback, then consider asking a representative group of staff members to read it and offer feedback. A quick online poll may work for busy colleagues.

Consulting with parents

Before consulting with parents, it's essential that they understand what PSHE is and why we teach it. If you can, get together a small group of parents and carers and try some of the activities already mentioned (such as what skills a Year Six child should have) before moving on to secondary schools and the differences between the parents' and carers' childhoods and their children's. Start a discussion on what children need now in order to thrive and stay emotionally safe in the future, and talk about how families and schools can play their part in supporting children.

Remind parents that this is a partnership – PSHE is one small part of the jigsaw of learning and should join seamlessly with parenting and other influences. You might like to chop the policy into separate parts and ask pairs or small groups of parents to read just part of the policy and give feedback on that. Can they understand it? Is it jargon-free? Does it make sense? Is it what they thought? Is there anything missing? Does it reflect the school's ethos?

Consulting with pupils

If you have a school council, or a group in which a mixed group of pupils meet, this could be a good opportunity to talk with them about the policy. If not, set up a focus group. Talk to them about what they think of PSHE and what they would like to learn about. Read some of the objectives and discuss these, as a whole group or in pairs, and check whether pupils feel these objectives accurately reflect their lessons. (Such discussions show the reason for making the objectives plain and simple.)

The pupils don't need to read or understand the whole policy, but this is a good opportunity to ask them what they like about PSHE, what they think about the content, how they learn, and whether they understand why they have PSHE lessons. Do they even know what the abbreviation stands for?

Consulting with governors

It's important that there is at least one governor who can champion PSHE. This may be the governor who leads on SEND (Special Educational Needs and Disability), child protection or behaviour, as PSHE may feel like a natural partner to these. Arrange to meet with this governor on a regular basis (at least once per term, and preferably face to face) to talk about any updates, changes and challenges. When it comes to reviewing the policy, this governor can provide support on the governing body by encouraging colleagues to read, think about and offer feedback on the policy.

Consulting with the wider community

Consider whether there are any key people in the wider community who need to be consulted. There may be faith leaders who contribute by delivering assemblies or enabling collective worship, school health professionals, local authority officers, after-school care providers, small-group or nurture-group providers, and so on. They may not need to read and give feedback on the whole policy, but it will be helpful to have their input on key areas.

Consulting with busy people

Think about how you can make consultation as simple as possible. If you can gather a group together for an hour, then you can cover a lot of ground. If not, consider face-to-face chat using video chat, or email or phone calls. Consider setting up an online poll. They are fairly straightforward to set up and you can add in closed questions (with *yes/no* answers), scales and open-ended sections so that respondents can add their own thoughts. Online polls pull together the information in a neat report.

Consulting with the wider school community is key for understanding and communication. It is a worthwhile step to take in order to move from a policy statement written by one person to a policy actively supported by the whole school community. Responses may include things you haven't thought of and may flag up misunderstandings or points that need clarification. If a suggestion is made that doesn't quite chime with (or even goes against) your aims for PSHE, then as a professional decide how you will respond. You don't necessarily need to change the policy, but this may flag up an area of misunderstanding that needs clarification, either within the policy or within the PSHE programme.

❋ SOMETHING TO THINK ABOUT

Check the next review date for your PSHE policy and start planning.

- Ask for staff meeting time to discuss PSHE with colleagues or lead an activity.

- Who will lead on writing, rewriting or reviewing the policy? Set some meetings in the diary.

- Decide how you will consult the wider school community, and who needs to be involved. Plan how you will do this over a period of time.

- Review your plan in the light of any responses or changes.

Take a look at the PSHE Association document *Creating a PSHE Education Policy in Your School*, which is available from the PSHE Association website: www.pshe-association.org.uk.

Starting points for PSHE

If you wish to refresh your school's PSHE programme of study, then you'll need to think about starting points. What do you know already about the needs of your pupils, and what else do you need to know?

If asked to describe your school and the needs of your pupils, you'll be able to do that fairly easily. You know this because you work with these pupils day in, day out, and because you know the school's prospectus and handbook and you know the school's data. It's important that the PSHE programme reflects the school as a whole and supports the overall learning and social ethos, rather than being something separate.

Looking at the academic progress and attainment data can help give you a picture of what happens across the school. You'll see if there are gaps in attainment, the sorts of groups of pupils who are succeeding, and whether there are any groups of pupils who need extra support. Look at the data about any particular groups of pupils who might perhaps need extra support in the form of PSHE sessions or where your planning needs to take account of particular sensitivities. Think about travellers, young carers, new arrivals and the newly bereaved. There may be areas of the curriculum that need to take into account sensitivities around all of these groups.

Behaviour records can tell you a lot about the sorts of behaviour incidents that occur in your school, how often these occur, when they happen and how they are dealt with. If there are a lot of behaviour incidents during lunchtimes or at playtimes, then think about how you deliver sessions on conflict management and assertive relationships. If there are incidents of pupils being rude to members of non-teaching staff, then consider how in PSHE you might help pupils develop empathy with these jobs. If lunchtime relationships or football rotas are a matter of concern, then ask the children to create solutions and to debate and discuss them during PSHE. In addition, look at any bullying incidents and patterns of behaviour. Perhaps Year Three needs some extra work on managing changing friendships or Year Six needs some time on developing responsibility and independence.

Participation in and attendance at extra-curricular activities can tell you a lot about the sort of pupils who are attending clubs. Look at the type of clubs and activities you offer and how elements of PSHE can be brought into these. In sports activities, do the sports leaders talk about the benefit of exercise and health, or offer opportunities for families to take part together? In after-school clubs, do the leaders provide healthy, nutritious meals in line with the school food policy, and does their behaviour management chime with the school's behaviour policy? In arts and crafts clubs, are leaders well trained in supporting pupils who might disclose personal concerns in a relaxed and informal atmosphere? Do they link the positive aspects of hobbies to positive mental health and wellbeing? Look at the gender balance of clubs and see whether there are equal numbers of boys and girls participating in sports and in arts- and crafts-based clubs. Do girls access clubs based on STEM (Science, Technology, Engineering and Mathematics) activities as much as boys? Are there any groups of pupils who are not able to access clubs and activities because of issues of timing or equipment? Check what sort of activities happen in the local community and try to make sure that those activities and yours don't clash.

● CASE STUDY

When a school did a survey of pupils attending their extra-curricular clubs they were dismayed to see a big drop off in boys attending after-schools clubs in Year Three. They stepped up their marketing materials for Wednesday afternoon football club and ran an assembly where pupils could demonstrate what they have learned in their clubs and encourage others to sign up, but it made no difference. At last the deputy head decided to talk to the parents of Year Three boys to find out what was happening and discovered that Wednesday afternoon was the local Beaver Scouts meeting. The following term they changed the day of some of their own clubs and sign-up increased.

PSHE adviser

Look at the take-up of school meals. Are all those entitled to a free meal taking it up? If not, are they bringing a nutritious packed lunch and do they have access to clean water? Are they allowed to sit with friends? The separation of packed-lunch and school-meal children at lunchtime can be a real bone of contention among younger children, so don't be afraid to use PSHE sessions with pupils to explore wider aspects of school life. Close links to the social aspects of eating together and the importance of eating a balanced meal can be addressed in PSHE.

You may have other data in your school that can inform your PSHE planning, such as school travel data, physical education data, pupil and parent annual questionnaires, and annual health or anti-bullying questionnaires. All of these can help you recognise the direction your PSHE sessions may need to take.

You can also collect 'soft' or 'perception' data. Simply talking with teaching and non-teaching members of staff can be really helpful. Perhaps teachers of certain year groups feel that their pupils need more support on managing friendships and bullying, or that sessions on puberty come too late in the year to make a real difference.

Running a focus group

Perhaps the easiest way to find out what is working and what isn't is to hold focus groups with small groups of pupils, yet we may not do this often enough. Focus groups can be used when teaching modules or when finding out what needs to be taught, for example in RSE.

Gather a group of no more than ten pupils, making sure that they are fairly representative of the class or year group as a whole (rather than a group of close-knit friends, for example, as they might have a similar outlook). Start with a chat or a very open-ended question so that they feel relaxed, and then ask them some key questions. Use a mixture of closed and open questions and jot down the answers. You might find it easier to record or video the group so that you can revisit the conversation afterwards. Explain that the recordings are for your own use only and remind pupils of confidentiality and safeguarding.

The following questions have been used with Year Six pupils for RSE. This is just one example; you can adjust the questions to suit your own school and your own pupils.

- Tell me about some of the sex-education lessons you've had at [name of school].

- What year were you in when you learnt about growing up and puberty? Was this the right age, do you think?

- What year were you in when you learnt more about adult relationships and how babies are made? Was this the right age, do you think?

- What have you learnt this year?/What are you going to learn in Year Six?

- Who taught those lessons?

- Who else might you like help from to teach these lessons?

- Tell me some of the facts you've learnt in RSE.

- Tell me some of the skills you've learnt in RSE.

- What sort of activities did you do? (For example, drama; worksheets; videos.)

- Were there any activities that didn't work for you? Why not?

- How did the school help your parents understand what you were learning?

- How could we make RSE learning even better for other pupils in the school?

- Is there someone you can go to if you have questions or concerns in relation to RSE?

- Is there anything else you want to tell me?

A more general discussion on PSHE might include questions like these:

- What do you understand about PSHE?

- What knowledge do you think PSHE should teach you?

- What skills do you think PSHE should teach you?

- What do you think a Year [—] pupil should learn about:

  - growing up, relationships and sex?

  - drugs and alcohol?

  - keeping healthy?

  - emotional health?

  - learning about money?

  - keeping safe and risky behaviours?

- What other topics do you think you should learn about in PSHE? (For example, media; body image.)

- How do you learn best in PSHE? (For example, practical activities; projects; theme days; speakers.)

- What resources would help you to learn? (For example, video clips; magazines; worksheets.)

- Anything else?

The above examples are for older pupils, but can easily be adjusted for KS1 or Early Years Foundation Stage (EYFS) pupils too.

Looking at local and national data

It's important to know what national and local data say about young people, too. Media outlets often report on wellbeing issues or new studies – but always look at the source materials themselves, not just the often sensationalised or cherry-picked headlines!

Teenage pregnancy data

Look at local trends in terms of under-18 conception rates to see whether your school is in a particularly vulnerable area. There are a wide range of factors associated with teenage pregnancy, not just poor RSE, but being aware of where your school sits in relation to these rates may help you to plan better. The Office for National Statistics (ONS) will have the latest national and regional figures, and local figures will be available from your local authority's public health lead or via the Joint Health and Wellbeing Strategy for your area. Under-18 conception rates are also part of the Child Health Profiles.

Child Health Profiles

Child Health Profiles are available by county or by borough on the Public Health England (PHE) website[2] and contain a RAG (Red, Amber, Green) rating for everything from GCSE attainment to dental health and Accident and Emergency admissions. These data are for a whole town or an area, but it's worth looking to see where the major

---

2   See http://fingertips.phe.org.uk/profile-group/child-health/profile/child-health-overview.

gaps are – and also where your local area is doing well. You can also interrogate these data and compare them with other areas.

NHS data

The NHS has a list of all the latest reports and data on aspects of wellbeing such as smoking, alcohol and tobacco use, and the National Child Measurement Programme.

There are a lot of data out there: the idea is to just have a better overview of the context of your schools and the community in which your pupils live. There's no need to preface every PSHE lesson with a shedload of data, but some data may help you in deciding what to teach, how and when. Do you live in an area of high under-18 conception? Make sure your RSE is robust and well resourced, and that pupils have access to any support they might need, both now and in the future. Are there higher levels of poor dental health in your area? How could you bring teaching about good dental hygiene and brushing into the curriculum? Could you arrange for a dentist to visit to talk to pupils and parents?

If key issues do emerge from the health data, then make sure these are flagged up in school policies too, as part of the introduction or in the aims and objectives.

It's important to remember that data, whether quantitative or qualitative, change over time and also that each year group can be different. By running occasional focus groups and chatting to all members of the school community – teaching and non-teaching staff, children, parents and governors – you will be better able to give substance and relevance to the PSHE programme.

Programming PSHE into a busy curriculum

There's no doubt that the primary curriculum is full to bursting. In addition to the National Curriculum subjects, there are booster groups, catch-up sessions, nurture and social groups, and music lessons – sometimes it can feel like a miracle when the whole class stays in one place for a whole lesson! In this busy world PSHE can easily drop off the curriculum or be squeezed so much that it ends up limited to just a few minutes here and there.

In an ideal world, PSHE would have a set session on the timetable once a week with a decent amount of time in which to deliver a full session. The time would be protected, and wouldn't be the first thing to go to make space for exam preparation or fire alarm practice. In reality, however, PSHE may be spread across two short sessions or one larger session every two weeks. It may be taught in half-termly modules, with children studying PSHE for one half of the term and another subject area for the other half. Even so, it's entirely possible to plan and teach effective PSHE in any of the above scenarios.

Some schools say that their PSHE is built into other subject areas and that the threads run throughout the school. I would argue that this is true of SMSC rather than PSHE, however. SMSC is the bedrock of all schools – the ethos of the school and the 'This is how we do things here' strand that makes your school unique. PSHE, however, is the explicit teaching and learning of PSHE skills, and while there are close links with other curriculum areas, and many opportunities to combine the two, there are also times when PSHE needs to be taught as a discrete subject.

In the next chapter we will look at the links between other subject areas and PSHE, but PSHE topics are not simply aspects of other National Curriculum subjects. Is there enough time in Science, for example, to explore fully the emotional and relationship aspects of RSE and to practise and develop skills relating to growing up? Also, if PSHE is seen as a facet of other subjects, it's trickier to demonstrate that the PSHE curriculum is being fully covered and to build in assessment.

If your school doesn't have separate sessions, however, then there must be clear mapping to show where PSHE teaching and learning is taking place. Teachers need to be aware where the line falls between the topic and the PSHE elements. Assessment opportunities need to be built in and the programme needs to be evaluated regularly by teachers and by the PSHE lead, to make sure that it is meeting the needs of the pupils.

If PSHE is split across the week in smaller sessions, then think about how to split lessons between two or three sessions rather than trying to cram too much into one session or ending up with only a quick circle time or discussion. In the first short session, set up the ground rules and introduce the topic; then deliver the main teaching activity. In the second session, recap on what you covered in the first, and then go straight into the learning activity or activities. Finish up with the plenary and/or assessment and reflection. If you have a small amount of time later in the week (such as lining-up time, a few moments before lunch, or break time), recap quickly on the learning and maybe talk together about an imaginary scenario. You could also finish the session or sessions with a takeaway message or a task for pupils to complete before next week's first session.

As an example, a short topic on 'Keeping clean' at Key Stage 1 might look like this ('think–pair–share' is explained in 'Using discussion techniques' in Chapter Four):

Monday (15 minutes): Recap on ground rules and introduce the 'keeping clean' topic. Use think–pair–share to get pupils to think of all the things that help keep us clean. Pairs feed back and teacher makes notes. Teacher asks pupils to look around their home and think of anything they may have missed out, ready for next session.

Wednesday (15 minutes): Quick recap on ground rules and the list of ways of keeping clean. Talk about why we need to keep clean and what might happen if we don't. Pairs are given a sheet divided into 'Morning', 'Afternoon', 'Evening' and 'Night', and draw and write the ways of keeping clean at each point of the day (e.g. Morning: brushing teeth; Afternoon: washing hands for lunch; Evening: bathtime; Night: brushing teeth again). Check understanding.

Friday (5 minutes before lunch): Teacher reminds pupils about washing their hands properly, and the class practise the movements together before washing their hands for lunch.

And here's a Key Stage 2 example:

Monday (15 minutes): Recap on ground rules and introduce the topic of 'assertive, aggressive and passive'. As a class, come up with descriptions of what each word means, and check understanding. Teacher gives a scenario and acts it out three different ways with a volunteer pupil – aggressive, passive, assertive. Teacher asks pupils to try to start being assertive in their interactions before the next session.

Wednesday (15 minutes): Recap on ground rules. Did anyone try out being assertive? How did it feel? Try out some superhero power poses together, to help pupils feel more confident and ready to try out some ideas. Give pairs some scenarios and ask them to act them out, as per the example on Monday. Teacher observes, supports, and checks understanding. End with a self-reflection (verbal or written).

Thursday/Friday (spare minute here and there): Teacher asks pairs to act out their three scenarios from the other day. (Two pairs demonstrating their scenarios could take no more than two minutes and teacher can be doing other simple tasks.) Ask pupils to practise their assertiveness skills in the coming week and to feed back each morning at registration time.

A few minutes here and there are not ideal, but PSHE can be taught flexibly and adapted to your school's routines. Most important is making sure that pupils are reminded to *apply* their PSHE learning across the week, so that they practise their skills in real situations.

In rare cases, schools have a specialist PSHE teacher, and pupils then have their PSHE lessons during the class teacher's Planning, Preparation and Assessment (PPA) time. Again, it's crucial that *all* staff know the content and learning of the PSHE lessons, so that they can remind pupils of what they've learned, encourage them to practise their skills, and show that they too value PSHE learning. The threads running through PSHE need to lead back every time to the classroom and to the pupils' lives. It's no good having a brilliant lesson on anti-bullying if the children then go out into the playground and spend lunchtime fighting each other!

However you plan your PSHE sessions, bear in mind the principles and practice of high-quality PSHE teaching and learning.

❂ SOMETHING TO THINK ABOUT

Reflect on how your school timetables PSHE and consider whether you get the most out of your sessions, without cramming too much in or skipping over key activities. Is there a way to better adapt to the time you have? Can you identify any brief moments of dead time (e.g. while lining up, during registration or at lesson changeover) when you could recap and reinforce PSHE messages?

The PSHE Association's *Scheme of Work Planning Toolkit for KS1 and KS2* comes with two curriculum overview examples. These can be downloaded from the PSHE Association website.

Creating cross-curricular links

However you choose to timetable PSHE at your school, mapping where PSHE occurs across the curriculum will ensure that there's no repetition and that the spiral curriculum builds and grows. It will also help ensure consistency in the message throughout the school.

It's a valuable exercise to ask subject leaders to identify themes in your school's subject programmes of study and to seek out areas of commonality. To start with, ask them to grab a highlighter and highlight the key areas identified where different subjects and PSHE overlap. As a longer-term project, consider tweaking areas of learning so that they reflect the aims and objectives of your PSHE policy and thus ensure that consistent messages emerge. Remember, though, that covering some areas of PSHE in other subjects is not the same as delivering well-planned discrete PSHE lessons, so this shouldn't take away from your PSHE curriculum. The aim is rather to strengthen the delivery and consistency of teaching and learning. Equally important, too, is how other subject areas impact on PSHE learning.

The following are some suggestions of ways in which PSHE might be linked into other curriculum areas.

English

There are clear links between PSHE and English in the Early Years Foundation Stage, through reading and exploring books. Most picture books and stories have some sort of moral message, and these messages can be simply linked back to real-life experiences. Identify which picture books and novels lend themselves to discussions on the behaviour and motivations of the characters. Use drama techniques such as hot-seating to encourage empathy and thinking around the bigger picture.

Writing too offers opportunities to link to the PSHE curriculum. Tasks around persuasive writing, writing for an audience, writing letters and writing in character can all be linked to topics being studied in PSHE. Consider making explicit links between the two subject areas using activities such as writing a letter to the council, for example about the lack of play areas in the local area, or developing a debate around whether or not boys and girls should wear the same uniform.

Mathematics

Make sure that messages given in Maths are consistent with the messages you give in PSHE. The obvious links are probably when collecting and organising data. With younger children it's tempting to use sweets as a way of demonstrating tallying and graph-making or as a concrete way of showing number operations or data collection, but this can be confusing if the PSHE messages are about healthier lifestyles and these are being contradicted in other subject areas. It's not about being a spoilsport or a party-pooper: it's about ensuring that PSHE has parity with other subjects and that the messages given in PSHE lessons are valued across the school.

There are also close links between money topics in Maths and PSHE. Both subject areas offer the opportunity to explore Maths in real-life situations, such as collecting money for charity through fundraising, creating enterprise activities, or managing a real-life budget for the school council or a class event.

Science

There are clear links between Science and PSHE in terms of topics about growing, changing and the physical characteristics that make us humans. Science can also provide the opportunity to explore issues around the effect of medicines on the body and how exercise and movement are an important part of living a healthy lifestyle. Link the changing and growing to the PSHE curriculum by developing skills around managing changing bodies, exploring ways of staying fit and healthy, and experiencing the emotional changes associated with growing up. (We'll look at these links in more detail in Chapter Three.)

Art and Design

In Art, as well as creating art themselves, children should learn about key artists and architects and their work. In terms of PSHE, this is an opportunity to link to the conditions in which they worked and their motivations and behaviour. Talk about how the social, political and historical context affected how these artists worked. Discuss how art reflects the cultural context of the artist and how artists express themselves through their craft. Why is it important to express our creativity? What are the links between positive mental health and creativity?

Design offers the opportunity to look at advertising and media and to consider how colour, design and language encourage us to respond to products.

Computing

When creating computer-based projects, make sure that messages are consistent. There are clear links between computer use, staying safe online and ways of behaving online: make sure that these are covered thoroughly in Computing and that the same messages are reiterated in PSHE. Many pupils will already be interacting online via game-playing; and many will already be using, or will soon be using, social media. The safety and behaviour rules need to be reiterated and explored in various ways, and Computing is an opportunity to revisit some of the threads running through PSHE, including communicating, resilience and risk-taking. Conversely, there are many opportunities for using technology in PSHE, and the use of technology should be seen as a normal part of lessons. Use photographs, video-recording, voice-recording, vlogging, apps and tablets.

● CASE STUDY ————————————————————————

I was working with a group of Year Six on risk-taking. As a warm-up game we did an activity on high risk/low risk. One of the scenarios I suggested was going to meet a child their own age in real life that they had met online. I put it in as a bit of a red herring as they had covered online safety over and over in this school. To my surprise half the group stood at the 'no risk' end. We had a discussion about the perceived risk and they were all clear that the person they were meeting might be an adult rather than a child and that they may be placing themselves in a dangerous situation. One child shrugged, 'If it turned out to be an adult, I'd just run away.' Another added, 'I'd bring a baseball bat.' We stopped the activity to discuss this further – would they be able to run away from a strong adult? Would it be safe to walk around with a baseball bat? Would a ten-year-old really be able to get away from a strong adult? This was a topic that definitely needed going over again. While the children knew about internet safety they hadn't made the link between that and their own safety.

PSHE adviser

Design and Technology

The Cooking and Nutrition strand has very close links with the PSHE curriculum. Ensure that messages are consistent between the two and that activities around cooking include selecting ingredients, exploring where food comes from, seasonality, growing, and simple budgeting (linked to Maths). Place cooking opportunities within the context of a healthy lifestyle and how to make healthier choices.

Geography

In Geography, there are links between human and physical geographical studies and PSHE. When looking at the local area, talk about how humans live and interact with the built environment. How do people stay healthy? What choice of shops is there? How do people work, play or worship together? How do people socialise, and are there places of nature and calm? How could the local area be made a better place for people's physical and mental health?

In terms of global geography, discuss how people adapt to their environment, how they live and work, and what foods they eat.

History

Social History has close links to PSHE in terms of what motivates people, how and why conflict erupts, and how different societies work.

Follow the development of health care through learning about Florence Nightingale and Mary Seacole, or discuss the political and social climates that led key figures such as Rosa Parks or Emily Wilding Davison to seek change. History lends itself to writing or acting in character and to developing an understanding of how and why people behave as they do. It also offers the opportunity to look at related areas, such as food and eating, and how people lived, worked and socialised.

● CASE STUDY

I was tasked with planning and teaching a Year Four topic on personal hygiene and teeth. As a PPA teacher this was my only contact with two classes, one of which was exceptionally challenging. Much of the required content was dull, and very similar to a previous topic that they had covered in Year Two. I decided to base the module around their topic of Tudors. Using historical examples we compared Tudor attitudes to health, hygiene and teeth to our own. It made it more fun for the children and helped cover any embarrassment some children felt about their own washing habits. We could use extreme examples of bad hygiene in a very impersonal way. The children engaged to an incredible degree. Their class teacher noticed the influence on their literacy work and on a trip to Hampton Court Palace. I will certainly use cross-curricular planning for difficult or dull PSHE topics in future.

PPA teacher

Languages

Apart from the obvious links of being able to converse about home, family and leisure activities, it's important to bring out the benefits of learning a new language. Being able to converse with someone who speaks that language opens up the world in terms of cultural understanding; it also creates potential career opportunities and brings greater confidence. In teaching Modern Foreign Languages (MFL), make sure that these benefits are highlighted and that the language is placed in its cultural, historical and social context.

Music

Exploring the way in which music communicates meaning is closely linked to PSHE learning. Looking at the way composers create feeling and mood in their music can have an effect on how we respond to it.

You could also look at how music can affect our mental health and wellbeing. For example, various studies have shown that singing promotes positive mental wellbeing, boosts mood and reduces stress.[3]

Physical Education

Bring out the need for exercise as an important element of living a healthy lifestyle, along with building physical fitness, strength, flexibility and resistance. Help children to understand the link between PE lessons and a lifelong love of physical activity.

Working together in a team is an important part of PE and PSHE, and activities that help build teamwork can be linked back to the classroom. Explore what makes a good team and the different roles that we each have to play.

There is also the opportunity to explore the importance of practice and of failing while practising, and to learn that failing is fine – what matters is that we had a go.

Threading key skills through your programme

If PSHE is a tapestry of topics linked through knowledge, skills and understanding, there are threads that pull the whole picture together. These threads should be at the heart of every PSHE lesson and activity and part of the spiral curriculum that gives consistency across your whole-school programme. When planning and delivering PSHE, think about how these threads are being taught and practised.

Communicating

Communication is the key underlying concept of all teaching and learning in PSHE. We communicate verbally and non-verbally, in real

---

3   For example, Clift, S., Hancox, G., Staricoff, R. and Whitmore, C. (2008) *Singing and Health: A Systematic Mapping and Review of Non-Clinical Research*. Canterbury: Sidney de Haan Research Centre for Arts and Health, Canterbury Christ Church University.

terms and online. The children now in schools will be spending more and more of their lives online, and although we don't exactly know what that online world will look like when they are adults, giving them the skills of effective communication will be key to future relationships. From the earliest age we need to be giving children the language and vocabulary to express themselves effectively, and this effective communication will help them manage relationships both now and in the future.

One aspect of communication that is often neglected is how to communicate assertively. Children also need to be able to recognise the difference between assertive, aggressive (including passive-aggressive) and passive communication. While you may not use the word 'assertive' with younger children, it's important that they begin to learn what assertive communication looks and feels like. Good communication includes listening, reflecting, thinking and expressing themselves, so PSHE lessons need to provide opportunities for children to practise these skills.

If you spend any time online, you'll have an understanding of how aggressive some communications can be. While it's good that we can all express ourselves on social media and share our ideas, thoughts and opinions, too many communications are unnecessarily angry and aggressive: 'I'm right, you're wrong, and you're a fool for holding that opinion.' It's rare to see a conversation where two people have differing standpoints, listen to each other's point of view, think about what is being said, and then either agree to disagree or consider whether there may be some shared middle ground between the two opinions.

Being *assertive* means being able to communicate your thoughts, feelings and opinions clearly and to state what you want, and do this in a clear, honest way that respects the other person. It can be challenging to communicate like this, so the more practice children have, the better they will become at it. (And as adults we too could all do with a bit more assertive communication in our lives.)

Aggressive communication can be verbal, non-verbal and physical. We feel bad, and by acting in an aggressive way we want to control, upset, anger or scare the other person and make them feel bad too. Think of the times you've been at the receiving end of aggressive behaviour and how it made you feel both physically and emotionally. The adrenaline will have started to flow, putting your body into a 'fight, fright or flight' mode, and it's a miserable feeling. Developing better communication skills – which includes developing empathy

– can help children understand that assertive behaviour is a more positive and effective way of communicating.

Under the 'aggressive' heading comes *passive aggression*. Passive-aggressive behaviour can include gossiping, spreading rumours, non-verbal actions like sighing or eye-rolling, or refusing to speak to someone. Being on the receiving end of passive-aggressive behaviour may leave you feeling helpless, and you may not even be sure what you've done to warrant the behaviour. Children may use passive-aggressive behaviour in leaving friends out, whispering about them, ignoring them and making them feel bad. They in turn may respond to passive aggression with overt aggression or by becoming passive. Passive aggression is a controlling behaviour: it needs to be explored in PSHE in a variety of ways so that children develop the skills to recognise the behaviour, to consider how to respond, and to think about why people may communicate in this way.

Passive behaviour involves taking the path of least resistance and not allowing your feelings to be taken into account. When faced with aggressive, passive-aggressive or even assertive behaviour, it is often easier to give in; but by giving in, the passive person won't have their needs met or their wants heard – in effect, they are putting others' wants and needs before their own. Again, this results in unequal relationships in which one party is happy and the other is not.

Practising these skills throughout the PSHE curriculum may have a payoff in other areas too. As adults, by *modelling* positive communication skills in school, we will help children develop their understanding of the benefits of effective communication.

Developing these skills can also help in managing conflict and friendship problems. Too often as adults we 'sort out' problems by giving a short-term solution. If two children have fallen out over a game, for instance, we might suggest that neither play the game, that one of them plays another game, that the children 'make up' and say sorry...or whatever else will 'sort out' the problem when we're already frazzled and have a thousand and one other things to sort out. Instead, in PSHE we can help children develop effective communication skills: they can try out scenarios and practise skills that can lead to a different way of managing simple conflict. Remind the children of the learning they've done in PSHE and ask them to come up with solutions themselves – solutions that mean that *both* parties are satisfied with the outcome. If you've been working on developing these communication skills from the earliest age, you'll find that even young children can talk and come up with possible solutions to a real-life problem. It's always tempting to step in as adults and sort out problems, but it's important to allow children the time and space to practise their skills in real-life situations too.

● CASE STUDY

I was teaching a Year Five group about the difference between assertive, aggressive and passive. We brainstormed words that described each behaviour (shouting, walking away, whispering, shrugging, speaking calmly, etc.) and then I gave pairs a short scenario. I asked the pairs to act the scenario out aggressively, then passively, then assertively. It was really interesting seeing how the children added in subconscious body language – when they were being passive they shrank and look cowed and when being assertive stood taller and straighter. One pair really struggled with an assertive outcome to their scenario and kept falling back into passive mode (that's okay, whatever you like, it's fine). As a group we talked about what the pair could do to be more assertive, and although it took a while, the pair eventually got it. It was obviously a challenge for both children to force themselves out of passive mode but they were able to describe how it felt different and how they would be able to recognise when they were being passive in the future.

PSHE adviser

Building resilience through PSHE

Resilience seems to involve several related elements. Firstly, a sense of self-esteem and confidence; secondly a belief in one's own self-efficacy and ability to deal with change and adaptation; and thirdly, a repertoire of social problem-solving approaches.[4]

---

4   Rutter, M. (1985) 'Resilience in the face of adversity: Protective factors and resistance to psychiatric disorder.' *British Journal of Psychiatry 147*, 6, 598–611.

Resilience is often described as 'bounce-back-ability', and the definition given above by Michael Rutter seems like a good place to start in terms of PSHE. Developing resilience is one of the threads running through PSHE, and giving pupils the skills to develop their resilience can be one of the protective factors in managing positive mental health.

Being able to make mistakes safely, to learn from them and then to move forward is one of the main factors of resilience. If a child is able to recover from disappointment or failure then they will be better able to cope with a complex and challenging world. To do this, however, pupils need to be able to feel that it's okay to try new things and be given a safe space in which to do so, but also to be challenged to develop their learning and to develop an emotional toolkit they can use in times of need.

Let's break Rutter's definition into its component parts.

'A sense of self-esteem and confidence'
Through PSHE, children can learn about teamwork, develop their own skills, reflect on their own feelings and thoughts, and develop confidence through learning new skills.

'A belief in one's own self-efficacy…'
Developing skills of communication and managing problems can help with this feeling of self-efficacy. If a child is learning to tie their shoelaces, it may often be easier to do it for them – it saves time and effort, especially if they're fumbling and getting frustrated. However, supporting the child and allowing them time to practise and develop their skills means that they won't need your help the next time. That may seem logical when we're talking about shoelaces, yet how often as adults do we sort things out, offer easy solutions and take the decision-making away from children? If we ask children how they sort out problems and the answer is always 'Tell the teacher', then perhaps we need to examine whether we're giving children the skills they need to manage their lives. The satisfaction of succeeding after trying and struggling is even greater *because* it felt challenging at the time.

'…and ability to deal with change and adaptation'
Children face a huge number of changes in their lives – a new class every year; going to secondary school; changing friendships and families; possibly facing loss for the first time. Others will experience

changes to their family set-up, moving home, arriving in the country, adapting to a new culture and language, and so on. For some, changing teacher at the beginning of the year can seem like a huge hurdle, as can struggling with a new concept in a subject area.

Developing skills around resilience means that children will have a better approach to change, being better able to express themselves. Some children tend to be worriers and will worry about not getting things right, so it's essential that PSHE lessons are a time when children feel safe to try out new ideas, express their opinions and be listened to.

'A repertoire of social problem-solving approaches'

Problem-solving should be at the heart of PSHE lessons, which is why the *skills* part is as important as the *knowledge* part. Using practical and engaging activities can help children find out what they're good at and what approaches might work best for them. Some of the activities in the section on best practice will help with this, as well as developing skills in effective communication.

Thriving

PSHE is one of the ways we can help children not just to cope or to survive but to *thrive*. Developing skills around managing feelings and developing confidence helps children to tackle life's challenges. When planning PSHE lessons, think about how the skills children develop in the lesson can help them thrive in the short term (today, this week, this month), the medium term (this term, this year, throughout primary school) and the long term (next academic stage, future life).

Exploring challenges and issues and developing healthy protective behaviours can help children to thrive in all aspects of learning. If a child feels safe, ready to learn and has a range of positive relationships to draw upon, then it stands to reason that they will be better able to learn and to make the best use of all teaching and learning opportunities.

Establishing a positive school ethos, in which learning linked to physical and emotional health is valued, can help pupils to thrive. PSHE is one of the elements where these elements can be thoroughly explored.

Challenging

Encouraging pupils to think for themselves, to evaluate and to reflect is another key thread running through PSHE, particularly when talking about social norms. In a world of 'fake news' and multiple sources of information, many of which are subjective or have an agenda or bias, it's important that children develop the skills to make decisions about what *they* think is right.

But 'challenging' is not just about what we ourselves do. Children need to develop their moral and ethical frameworks, and this may include challenging others' misconceptions or views while respecting that others may have strong feelings or reasons for holding those views. In the previous chapter we looked at difference and diversity in PSHE and the importance of encouraging pupils to be open-minded, to challenge accepted social norms and to create their own moral frameworks within the parameters of family, community and culture. Developing skills in critical thinking and listening are part of being able to challenge social norms and are an important part of communicating effectively. These skills will also help children manage the overload of information and will help them prepare for messages later on about issues such as body image, gender difference and healthy relationships.

Managing risk

Managing risk is part of the teaching and learning in PSHE, just as risk is an inherent part of life. Every day we make hundreds of decisions that involve physical and emotional risk-taking: crossing the road, driving a car, starting a new relationship, buying a property, or selecting a snack. This is where PSHE needs to move away from giving knowledge and handing down wise advice to helping children look at issues in a meaningful way so that they can explore all sides and then make up their own minds. Children need to consider the often subtle differences between an *unsafe* risk (crossing a busy street without looking, taking a dangerous dare, taking a medicine without adult supervision) and a *safe* risk (speaking in front of the class, starting a new skill or hobby, chopping vegetables under adult supervision), as well as how to turn an unsafe risk into a safe risk, depending on age and ability.

All risks have consequences, so exploring what these consequences may be and learning how to minimise negative consequences are essential parts of teaching and learning. Children need to practise recognising risk, discussing and assessing risk in a variety of situations, and making decisions. They also need to learn about when they may need to call upon help and how to do this. (This includes contacting the emergency services and sources of support such as Childline.)

Some children will be nervous of ever taking risks and some will jump in without thinking about consequences: in striking a balance by discussing and exploring various risky situations you will help both sides to develop their recognition and management of risk.

Tom Senninger developed a 'learning zone' model[5] which, although developed to describe learning, can also be useful with children when thinking about safe and unsafe risk. It provides a clear visual reference of three concentric circles nestled one within another. At the centre is the *comfort zone*, around this the *stretch zone* or *learning zone*, and the outer circle represents the *panic zone*.

- The *comfort zone* is where we feel at home. It's safe and familiar and we operate happily within its boundaries. In terms of risk, this might be something like eating a favourite food or playing with a best friend.

- The *stretch zone* involves taking a safe risk, but a risk all the same – trying a new food, perhaps, or making a new friend. This area is also called the *learning zone* as we only learn and get better at something when we take a (safe) risk, such as taking the next step in a hobby or skill-based activity, talking to someone we don't know, or walking to the shop on our own.

- The *panic zone* elicits the fight or flight response, and it's a warning sign that we might be about to take an unsafe risk. Unlike the anxious or butterfly feeling of the stretch zone, this is a definite 'no' zone: it's time to stop and look at what it is that's making us panic. There may be a risk involved that is definitely unsafe (giving your address to a stranger you meet online, drinking alcohol with older friends, climbing a high fence), or it may be that the risk can be made into a safe one. The important aspect is that the panic zone should make us stop

---

5   See www.thempra.org.uk/social-pedagogy/key-concepts-in-social-pedagogy/the-learning-zone-model.

and assess the risk and make a decision based on what we know and the skills we may need to employ.

Recognising and managing risk is a thread that runs through every topic of PSHE: the more that children get the opportunity to practise their skills in recognising, assessing and managing risk, the better equipped they will be to meet life's challenges.

Seeking help

As we have limited time and resources in school, children may need to know how and where to seek further help, so including this thread in all lessons is crucial. They need to know whom they can talk to in school, and when and where; whom they can talk to at home; how they can access specialised help (school counsellor, school nurse, inclusion manager, teaching assistant, and the like); and where they can access anonymous support (such as Childline).

A simple age-appropriate reminder built into every lesson at plenary time may be enough, but children also need to know how to ask for help when they need it and how to recognise when they might have further questions. At the beginning of a module or topic, ask pupils to come up with some questions about it they'd like to ask, and then consider whether these will be addressed in the following lessons. If not, let children know if and when they *will* be addressed or − if they won't be − that they need to talk to someone else, such as their parent or carer. (There is more about answering children's questions in Chapter Three.)

● CASE STUDY ────────────────────────

A school was aware that the Key Stage 1 children often gravitated towards teaching assistants, office staff and midday staff if they had worries or concerns but weren't always confident of their names. The school took photos of all the key members of staff that children might come across in the day and made simple diagrams with pictures for every class door at child height. The children could refer to the pictures either to remind themselves of the names of staff or to point to the person they'd like to talk to or who helped them. While not directly part of a PSHE lesson it did mean that children knew there were several adults willing to help them in school and it also helped create stronger relationships between support staff and children.

PSHE advisor

✳ SOMETHING TO THINK ABOUT

When planning your PSHE lessons, think about these threads which run through the teaching and learning:

- Communicating
- Building resilience
- Thriving
- Challenging
- Managing risk
- Seeking help

You may not find all of them in every lesson, but think about how you plan to address them both within and outside PSHE lessons. How can you encourage children to apply and practise their learning and skills in a variety of situations at school?

Building a PSHE lesson from the ground up

By now you'll have a good understanding of what your pupils need to learn and how this fits into the curriculum as a whole. You'll understand the needs of the pupils in your school and you'll have built, or be thinking about building, a spiral curriculum based on those needs.

But it's Sunday evening and you're expected to teach a certain topic in PSHE to your class this week. You need to put together a lesson plan that engages and interests the pupils in your class, that stimulates learning, that addresses need and that ensures the learning has taken place.

If the lesson is part of a module or a set of lessons, think about what learning should have taken place by the end of the module and work backwards. For example, if by the end of five sessions you want children to have an understanding of loss and change, then break down what that might look like step by step and identify what you'll need to cover:

- *What knowledge might they need?* For example, that living things die and that we don't always know when that will happen; that we may experience grief, bereavement and loss in different ways; that there are ways of remembering a person who has died or left; that we may experience a range of different feelings; that others may experience loss in different ways; that some changes are reversible and some are not.

- *What skills do we want children to learn?* For example, how to recognise and name difficult or uncomfortable feelings; where to access and ask for support; techniques that can help us feel more positive; how to start a difficult conversation; how to help others who are experiencing loss.

- *What attitudes might we address?* For example, loss and bereavement in different cultures; the range of emotions and reactions following loss; expectations and empathy.

The above example might be used in Key Stage 1 or 2 – in making such a plan, you will need to take into account the experiences, age and prior learning of your pupils.

There needs to be a certain amount of input and teaching, so think about how to introduce the topic. In the first session you'll need to introduce or recap on the class ground rules. You could use a picture book, a film clip, a piece of music or a photograph to stimulate discussion and an assessment technique to establish what pupils already know and what they need to find out.

Think of where you will use whole-class, group or individual activities, and why. Are you putting the children in groups because that's what you always do? Might there be a more effective way of approaching this task? Plan a mix of activities that strike a balance between being teacher-led and encouraging pupils to practise and develop new skills. Do you want higher-energy activities, such as 'Agree/Disagree' corners, or problem-solving in a speed-dating format, or a more low-key approach with quieter, reflective activities, such as making a memory paper chain? How will you build assessment into these activities? Will you also assess progress and skills development at the end of the lesson, possibly with an 'I can' activity or a graffiti wall? (These activities are explained in detail in Chapter Four.) In the plenary, how will you check understanding and address any questions or misconceptions? Is there a final wrap-up activity such as a story, a reflection or a game?

Taking the lesson on loss and change as a starting point, a lesson might look like the one in the example below.

● EXAMPLE

The following is a simple bullet-pointed outline for teaching a lesson on loss and change:

- Recap on the class ground rules; then explain that in the next few PSHE sessions you'll be looking at different types of loss and change. Suggest avenues of support if children feel worried or overwhelmed at any point.

- Ask the class to listen to a sad piece of music, such as the 'Lacrimosa' from Mozart's *Requiem*, and then ask for words and phrases to describe the music. 'How did the voices and instruments change during the piece?' 'What did it make you think of?' 'What did the composer want to say with this piece?'

- Talk about how loss and change are a natural part of life and that we may have mixed feelings about this. 'What sort of feelings might we have?' 'What do these feelings look like, feel like and sound like?' 'How do we know if someone else is having these feelings?'

- Ask them to think about a time when something changed in their life and to talk to the person next to them about what happened, how it felt and what they did.

- Pull together some ideas about how to cope with changes, and who they could go to for help.

- Give pupils strips of coloured paper and pens and ask them to write or draw a time when change happened in their lives. Ask a few children who are willing to do so to share what they drew or wrote. Link and stick the strips together to form a paper chain. Explain that we all experience loss and change and that it's okay to have uncomfortable feelings.

- For plenary time, read out a scenario about change. This could be something you've made up ('Omar has just arrived in this class. He doesn't know anyone and he stands alone at playtime. One day you see him crying and he says that he misses his old school and his old friends. What might you say or do?') or it could be based on a character in a book that the class knows well. Make sure the scenario isn't based on anyone's personal story but reflects the sort of situations the children might come across.

- End by asking each pupil to complete an 'I know, I can, I understand' slip of paper to go in the 'I can' can.

- Recap on today's learning and say how that will lead into the next lesson.

Or, if time is short:

- Recap on the ground rules and explain what the children will be learning today.

- Listen to the music and have a group discussion on words and feelings in terms of loss and change.

- Brainstorm some strategies to support someone who is experiencing loss or change.

- Complete the paper chain activity and share some of the ideas. What advice might be given to this person?

- Ask pupils to complete an 'I can' statement. Recap on the day's learning and say how it will lead into the next session.

With a wide range of activities for delivering content and a range of assessment ideas, it's possible to create an active and engaging lesson or set of lessons for any topic. Remember the guiding principles of

PSHE and what constitutes good practice, and always keep in mind safeguarding and the need to signpost support.

Whether you're planning an hour-long or a 15-minute session, bear the checklist below in mind. It will be helpful whether it's a lesson you've planned, a lesson that has been planned by someone else or a commercially produced lesson plan.

● CHECKLIST: PLANNING SESSIONS

- Have I completed some sort of baseline assessment or assessment of learning before starting this lesson?

- How do I know that this topic is important for the pupils in my class to learn?

- How does this learning fit into our planned programme of PSHE? How does it link to other curriculum areas?

- Have I planned a range of activities that engage and challenge pupils' thinking?

- Have I made sure that pupils are learning skills as well as knowledge? Are there opportunities to explore attitudes and values?

- How can children use the knowledge and skills in their lives, either at school or at home? Is learning contextualised?

- Have I been sensitive to the needs of particular pupils in my class?

- Have I signposted further sources of support, such as people who can help at school or home, and local or national services?

- Have I created a safe learning environment in which pupils are able to practise new skills, ask questions and make mistakes without fear of being judged?

- Have I assessed learning and progress? Do I know what I need to do in the next lesson?

And here are some questions to ask yourself after teaching PSHE:

● CHECKLIST: REVIEWING SESSIONS ─────────

- What went well? What didn't go so well?

- What changes might I make if I were to teach this lesson again?

- Did this lesson meet the learning objectives and did pupils meet the success criteria? How do I know? Do I have any evidence of this through pupils' work (e.g. verbal, written)?

- Do I need to recap on anything in the next lesson?

- Did I answer all of the questions and address any gaps in knowledge?

- Do I have any additional training needs?

- Is there someone I can talk to if I need some extra support?

- What do I need to do next?

Using resources and schemes of work

Teachers and PSHE leads often ask for recommendations for schemes of work and it's not surprising. Wouldn't it be easier if there were just one scheme that could be rolled out across the schools that would fulfil every PSHE need so that you never had to do any planning ever again? There are schemes and resources galore available, but if there's one key message about PSHE, it's that it must address the needs of the pupils in *your* school – and every school is unique. So how do you marry both of these without having to create an entire programme of study, complete with lesson plans, from scratch?

Even if you choose to adopt a scheme of work in its entirety, it needs to be right for your school and it must be rolled out carefully with training for all of the staff involved in presenting it, so that they understand their roles in PSHE. You also need to consider the broader aspects of PSHE, such as the threads that run through it, including how and when these are taught, and the additional aspects of PSHE discussed in Chapter Five. If not carefully and thoughtfully used, the expensive resources will end up as a set of dusty tomes on a shelf. Before buying into any scheme, therefore, do the groundwork. Look at what is in the school already, what works for *your* children, and *your* curriculum approach to PSHE. Think about the topics and approach that will work with what you know about your pupils (see the earlier section about starting points) and how you will match this to staff training and ongoing support. Once it has been rolled out across the school, how will the delivery and impact be monitored and evaluated? How will annual training and support be delivered? Will you be able to do this in-house or is ongoing support part of the package? What additional training needs might you have?

There is a wealth of material available for PSHE, including commercially produced resources, textbooks and lesson packages; free resources from corporations and companies fulfilling their Corporate Social Responsibility (CSR); and resources from charities produced to support learning about their cause, which may include fundraising and awareness-raising opportunities. There are also peer-created resources available on a variety of websites, including the *Times Education Supplement* (TES) website, either free or for a small cost. Of course, not all resources are of equal quality, and whereas some will have been created with the PSHE Association's principles of PSHE in mind, others won't.

Resources may also come from visits and from visitors. Theatre in Education (TIE) companies often provide workshop materials or follow-up lessons, and there may be resources from visits that you can use in school afterwards. You might also have access to materials produced by your Local Authority or by faith schools – if so, check that they address the needs of your pupils and identify any gaps in learning that will need additional support.

The PSHE Association has a wide range of resources that have been given their Quality Mark. To gain the Quality Mark, resource producers go through a rigorous process which ensures that the resources meet the requirements of good practice. If a resource has the Quality Mark you can be sure that it reaches this high standard. Even so, check that it matches the needs of your pupils and fits well with your spiral curriculum and your whole-school approach to PSHE.

If you are selecting a resource to be part of your PSHE scheme of work that does *not* have the PSHE Association Quality Mark, consider the checklist below when assessing its quality.

● CHECKLIST: ASSESSING QUALITY

- *Why this resource?* Does it address a specific need in your curriculum? How do you know? If you've done the groundwork and have a good idea of what you want to teach and when, then consider whether this resource is the best way of delivering the topic.

- *Could you do it better?* Do the suggested activities engage children in active learning or are there vague suggestions about drawing posters, making leaflets or filling in worksheets? (All of these activities are valid, but they can get repetitive and can act as time-fillers when a better-planned activity could deliver the outcomes in a better way.) If you could do better, switch the activities up and personalise them for your pupils.

- *Are they age-appropriate?* Resources may specify a Key Stage or they may be age-specific, but even so, consider whether they address the needs of the pupils in your school or class. Does the lesson build on previous learning and fit into your school's spiral curriculum?

- *Does the lesson address the knowledge, skills and under-standing aspects of PSHE?* Beware resources that seem too knowledge-based, or adapt them to include activities that help pupils develop and practise their skills. Are there opportunities to discuss, think and reflect?

- *Is there a hidden agenda?* If the resource is commercially produced, is there an underlying message about enrolling with that bank, raising money for that charity or shopping at that store? As the teacher, it's for you to decide what messages you want your pupils to receive, which resources are appropriate for them and which chime with the ethos of the school.

- *Do the lessons follow good PSHE principles and practice?* Do they have a teacher guide that gives you background information and signposts further information? Do they have clear objectives and outcomes? And assessment opportunities? Do they link with current good-practice guidelines from the PSHE Association?

- *Are they up to date?* PSHE is a fast-moving subject area and things change quickly. Does the resource contain up-to-date information on the topic? If you aren't sure, match it up with the information on a recommended website or the latest government guidelines. Some topics change especially quickly, such as drug and alcohol information, and learning may be linked to national law and to guidance such as the Psychoactive Substances Act 2016 and may need to use newer terminology (e.g. replacing phrases like 'legal highs'). Check also that the resource doesn't fall into the trap of using outmoded practices or old-fashioned learning styles.

- *Does the resource match the aspiration and challenge of other teaching materials?* Or is it full of vague messages or suggestions of activities that may be fun to do but that won't help develop children's learning in the area?

- *Is there any additional training and support that your teachers need?* If the resource is new to the school and the topic is one the teachers haven't yet taught, make sure there is support in place to help them, such as training, staff meetings, local leads or advisers, articles, podcasts, websites, Teachmeets (meetings where teachers share good practice) or Pedagoos (communities of teachers sharing effective approaches to education). Schools can now access training and support in a wide range of ways.

- *Are there opportunities for parental involvement and feedback?* Can you share learning with parents and carers? How will you tell them about what their children are learning in PSHE?

Ultimately, the key questions are these: 'How does this resource add value to the curriculum?' and 'Could I do it better?'

✷ SOMETHING TO THINK ABOUT

Go through the resources you already have in school or class. Throw away or recycle any that are out of date or that don't meet the needs of your pupils.

Then check that the remaining resources meet your school's planned PSHE curriculum. Make a note of any gaps or topics that would benefit from new resources. If you find some, first check the PSHE Association website for materials with the Quality Mark – is there anything that meets your needs?

Chapter Three

TEACHING AND LEARNING IN PSHE

In this chapter we'll be looking at what works in PSHE and how to ensure that all lessons reflect the PSHE Association's 'Ten Principles of PSHE Education' (see the Appendix). These principles are based on good practice, research and experience in teaching PSHE, and form the cornerstone of all PSHE teaching and learning. We'll also cover some of the bigger, trickier topics, which may seem scary at first but which, once broken down and when taught with key techniques at your fingertips, can lead to some of the most rewarding sessions in PSHE. There are lots of examples and ideas to try out, all of which have been tested in the classroom and developed with pupils and PSHE experts.

Teaching and learning in PSHE: What works and what doesn't

Sometimes it's hard to know whether you're on the right track. If we talk too much about bullying, will that encourage pupils to try it? If we don't talk enough about mental health, will pupils struggle to recognise their feelings? Looking at some best practice in teaching and learning in PSHE will help you to frame lessons and provide support when tricky topics arise in class.

Shock tactics

While it may be tempting to show children horrific photographs of illnesses, diseased lungs and injured people when going for the short, sharp shock approach, such pictures tend to shock and upset them without having the desired long-term effect of acting as a deterrent. Shocking photos tend to be at the extreme end of the scale, so it's easy to think: 'That will never happen to me.'[1] The same goes for films and theatre shows which may act as triggers for some pupils. Think carefully about showing anything that depicts sexual violence, for example, or extreme forms of bullying.

Instead...
Introduce key facts and then discuss, debate and explore the topic from all sides. Look at the risks involved and encourage pupils to think about keeping safe, managing risk and seeking help when they need it.

Personal stories
Try to avoid 'It happened to me' stories in PSHE and do not use real examples of things that have happened in school. If children talk about specific incidents that have happened to them or other children in school, refer to your class ground rules. If you teach any sessions in reaction to incidents that have happened in school, always be sensitive to any pupils in the class who may have been personally involved.

Instead...
Use distancing techniques. Devise simple example scenarios, and use books and stories or characters that all pupils will know. Younger children will respond to puppets and picture books, or you could use a photograph as a stimulus.

Just say no to 'Just Say No'
The 'Just Say No' approach made famous by Nancy Reagan, America's former First Lady, came to the UK by way of the *Grange Hill* kids in the 1980s. The young actors from the television series fronted a campaign against drugs based on a key storyline and 'Just Say No' became the anti-drug strapline for a generation.

---

1   Research from: PSHE Association (2016) *Key Principles of Effective Preventive Education.* London: PSHE Association on behalf of the Child Exploitation and Online Protection Centre (CEOP).

Unfortunately, the 'Just Say No' approach really didn't work as a preventative strategy because it didn't support young people in understanding exactly *why* they were saying no. The main question was this: if drugs, alcohol and smoking are so bad, then why do people take drugs, drink alcohol and smoke? In the US, where the 'Just Say No' strategy was widely adopted, drug-enforcement officers visited schools to warn them of the dangers of drugs, but data showed that drug use among young people did not go down. What the programme failed to do was to help young people develop the skills associated with having social relationships and making choices.

Similar evidence has emerged around programmes that advocate total abstinence from sexual relationships. While it's important to teach children to be able to say 'No' and to be assertive and resilient, as a single strategy for preventing harm 'Just Say No' can become just a well-intentioned slogan.

Instead...
Focus on the skills that pupils will need in making their own decisions and on what may influence these decisions. When talking about drugs and alcohol, for example, ensure that pupils have access to relevant knowledge and that they understand the difference between legal and illegal drugs and know that all drugs can be harmful if taken incorrectly. As always, the emphasis should be on staying safe, managing risk and making decisions.

Preaching or teaching?
In a similar vein to 'Just Say No' and shock tactics, PSHE shouldn't be a lesson in finger-wagging. PSHE is about helping pupils to develop the skills of decision-making and giving them the tools to manage their lives and to thrive. Everyone makes mistakes, but we can support pupils in staying safe and in making informed decisions around risk.

Instead...
As a teacher, you yourself don't have to be a saint – it's far more important that you are human, approachable and supportive.

Don't forget, though, that you won't be sharing any dark secrets (no personal stories!) and your job as a teacher is to lead, to facilitate and to support learning. That is why it is important not to deliver

PSHE simply as knowledge. Pupils need information, but they need to process it in conjunction with developing the skills they need to keep themselves safe and to manage risk. Make sure your PSHE programme has plenty of opportunities for pupils to practise skills of effective communication, making decisions, managing relationships and accessing support when they need it.

Facts and more facts

When in doubt – especially with a topic with which you're not confident or familiar – it's tempting to stick to the facts. In this way drug education, for example, can end up being a long list of drugs, their effects and their dangers, and RSE can end up being a list of changes that happen in puberty.

Instead...

PSHE needs to be a balance of knowledge, skills and the exploration of attitudes and understanding. Lay the groundwork by finding out what pupils know already, what they need to know, and the skills they might need in the future.

Build lessons that include a wide variety of activities to build confidence, practise key skills and explore values and attitudes. For example, a lesson on healthy lifestyles might include some factual information about foods and activities that help us to keep healthy and then some problem-solving activities or some scenarios where pupils can test out their newly acquired knowledge. Add in opportunities to consider the pros and cons of healthy lifestyles, and check understanding through assessment. Offer opportunities across school to practise and explore these ideas further so that learning is consistently applied. For a truly joined-up approach, link healthy lifestyles to school-meal provision, snacks in school and after-school provision and clubs.

PSHE as a bolt-on activity

The curriculum is crowded and busy, and PSHE can often seem like the poor cousin to other subject areas. It's no wonder that pupils and teachers may see PSHE as an added extra which doesn't always have relevance to the curriculum or indeed their lives.

Instead...

Look at the PSHE curriculum in your school and consider whether it is serving the needs of your pupils. Has it remained the same for years or have you adapted and tailored it to the needs of your school? Is it referenced in other subject areas within the wider curriculum? Remember the links between attainment, progress and PSHE. Make sure that learning isn't confined to PSHE lessons. Check that the messages are consistent and embedded across the whole-school curriculum and ensure that learning is regularly reviewed in the light of new guidance, the changing needs of your school and your school ethos. In order to give coherence and consistency, the messages given in PSHE should be reflected in all subject areas and in extra-curricular activities.

❋ SOMETHING TO THINK ABOUT

Check your PSHE programme and make adjustments if necessary to ensure that good practice is always followed in PSHE teaching and learning.

Read the PSHE Association's 'Ten Principles of PSHE Education' (see the Appendix) and check that these apply to your school's PSHE programme.

Creating a triangle of knowledge, skills and understanding

Knowledge may well be power, but without practising related skills and developing associated understanding it's not going to be much of a life skill. Of course we want children to learn key facts and develop their knowledge – that's what schools are there for, after all – but if they can't apply this knowledge to their own and others' lives then we've missed an opportunity.

Finding this balance in PSHE is crucial – if we don't, children will have a stack of knowledge but without a full understanding of why or how to use that knowledge. Ask a child how many pieces of fruit and vegetables we should eat each day. Most will proudly reply 'Five' and hold up five fingers. The knowledge of the government's recommendations has sunk in and the answer is instant. We can cheerfully tick the box that says 'Teach children about healthy eating'.

Let's delve deeper, though: can that child who answered 'Five' say what sorts of fruits and vegetables count and describe portion sizes? Have they had the opportunity to taste a variety of fruits and vegetables? Have they had the opportunity to make some simple recipes that include fruit and vegetables? Have they visited a local shop to see where to buy them? Have they practised designing simple meals and balanced diets that include fruit and vegetables? In other words, have they really made the connection between the words ('Eat five a day') and the actions (eat five a day)?

In relation to behaviour, most children can tell you that bullying is unkind, that we shouldn't do it and that we must report bullies. Tick! But unless those same pupils can also recognise a wide variety of behaviours, develop the skills of empathy (so that they understand how a bullied person feels, and perhaps how a bully feels), and experience managing conflict and being assertive, then the words remain just that.

PSHE lessons still too often revolve around knowledge. In Ofsted's *Not Yet Good Enough* report (2013),[2] inspectors found that PSHE lessons around RSE, drug and alcohol education and keeping safe often relied on mechanics and didn't go into the skills pupils need to manage risk, change and relationships. In other words, they didn't address the skills threads running through the subject.

PSHE lessons need to be planned so that they develop a triangular approach of *knowledge, skills* and *understanding.*

The *knowledge* is the teaching part: it must be age-appropriate, it must contain enough rigour and challenge to make it relevant to the pupils' needs, and it must be factually correct. Lack of knowledge on the part of the teacher should never be a barrier to effective PSHE teaching. Check the facts by using information from a reputable website, ensuring that it is up to date, that it follows the latest expert guidance and that it uses the correct terminology.

There needs to be an opportunity then for children to explore their *understanding* of the topic and to look at attitudes and values around that topic. Use discussion, debate, four corners, conscience corridors, graffiti walls, scenarios, stories, film or research to help children think more widely around the topic. Taking the bullying example, children might listen to a story about a bullying incident and then discuss the

---

2   Ofsted (2013) *Not Yet Good Enough: Personal, Social, Health and Economic Education in Schools – Personal Social and Health Education in English Schools in 2012.* London: Ofsted.

different characters and what they could or might do. Perhaps you could then use four corners to decide how to deal with bullying or hot-seat the bully and the person who was bullied to find out why and what happened. By encouraging children to explore the wider issues you'll help them develop empathy and understanding about why people, including themselves, act the way they do – and how to change that behaviour if necessary. This is not about forcing all children into thinking the same way or becoming clones, but if they explore the nuances of topics themselves then they will be better equipped to make decisions and choices.

The third corner of the triangle is the need for children to practise and develop their *skills*. This is perhaps the most important but often most under-represented part of PSHE. PSHE lessons should be a safe place in which children can try out new skills – where they can fail, succeed and practise – before they meet the same issue in the real world. Take the bullying example again: skills development might be based around using scenarios, a film clip, a photograph or a story book that you had used earlier as a stimulus. Children could take part in a drama activity where they take on different characters in the scenarios; they could draw or write their advice; they could write a letter from the point of view of the bullied person or the bully; or they could give advice to the bullied person. In other words, there is a range of activities that enable children to experience genuine feelings in the safe environment of the PSHE class.

Let's take a sample anti-bullying lesson:

- The lesson starts with a discussion about bullying and the children all agree that bullying is unkind.

- The teacher reads a book and asks children what they think should happen. They agree that the bullied character should tell a teacher and that the bully should be punished.

- Pupils then create a poster that includes a slogan about reporting on bullying.

- In the plenary, the pupils show their posters and slogans and recap on what bullying is and how to report it.

The above is an adequate and fairly common PSHE lesson, but the skills and understanding could be drawn out more completely in order to make the lesson more meaningful and to engage pupils fully. Let's start again:

- The lesson starts with a recap of ground rules and the teacher reminds pupils that there are trusted adults they can talk to if they are worried.

- The teacher uses a puppet, a story or a scenario to introduce a story about bullying, and uses a four-corners activity to elicit initial ideas and thinking and to establish a baseline of understanding.

- Children write as many unkind and hurtful words, phrases and actions as they can think of inside a paper heart and share some of these in pairs.

- They then scrunch up the hearts and try to smooth them out again. The heart will never be as smooth as it was before the unkind words, and acts as a visual reminder of the lasting effects of bullying.

- In pairs, pupils take turns being an adult and a pupil who is reporting bullying. They use some of the words, phrases and actions from the heart activity. Can they explain how the bullying made them feel? Can the child playing the adult offer suitable advice?

- Each child makes a personal promise on a small heart that is theirs to take away.

- They repeat the four-corners activity: the teacher checks whether attitudes and understanding has progressed and addresses any misconceptions and questions.

- Finally, the teacher reminds pupils of where to go for help, both within and outside school, and reminds pupils to keep their personal promises throughout the week.

The second lesson example can still be done in the classroom with the same minimal resources, but it contains additional opportunities for children to think, consider, practise and explore. It has simple assessment opportunities built in and encourages children to think beyond the classroom. While the heart activity may seem a bit cheesy, the fact that it's a concrete, tangible device gives it more impact than discussion alone.

The above examples don't give ages – this lesson or something similar could be delivered from Reception to Year Six, with tweaks depending on age and understanding. With younger pupils you might use a puppet with a problem or a picture book; with older pupils you might use a more nuanced story, scenario or film clip, such as BBC Learning's animated 'Primary Mental Health films'.[3] (Always check first that resources are appropriate for the age and level of understanding of your pupils.)

Whether you're using a commercially produced lesson plan, a peer-produced plan or your own plan, it's essential that you analyse them for the different elements. Do lessons contain opportunities for exploring understanding and for developing attitudes and skills? If not, what can you add to the lesson plan to give it more balance?

Covering key topics in PSHE

The topics that come under the banner of PSHE can seem to expand and expand. In the last few years we've been told that schools should teach happiness, grit, character, resilience, work skills, cooking, parenting, first aid and road safety – the list goes on and can seem huge and very abstract. If we taught all these topics we'd have no time to teach anything else, and there's only so much time in the school day! In addition to this list we also have our statutory duties around Safeguarding, SMSC and Prevent.

Schools, however, are only one part of the puzzle. While it can seem that schools are seen as the answer to all society's ills and that teachers should also be expert social workers, mental health coaches and psychotherapists, there is only so much we can do. We need to remember that we're only one part of the puzzle of a child's life and focus on what we can realistically teach with the time, resources and expertise we have.

It's even more important, therefore, that the PSHE curriculum is carefully planned to address the needs of the pupils in your school and built around the skills threads. It can be hard to resist

---

3   BBC Learning, Primary Mental Health films: 'Being a bully – Ariana's story' and 'Being bullied – Jake's story': www.bbc.co.uk/programmes/p05c3byd.

the latest ideas, suggestions and trends. It is better, however, to be proactive and to consider what is best and what works, based on clear evidence and research rather than on whatever is the latest zeitgeisty headline grabber.

Rather than suddenly introducing lessons on character and grit or mindfulness, it is better to unpack these topics and to consider how the concepts might be taught through the medium of a well-planned PSHE curriculum.

The PSHE Association has divided PSHE teaching and learning into three core themes, which form a strong base on which to start building your PSHE programme. The three themes are:

- Health and wellbeing

- Relationships

- Living in the wider world – economic wellbeing and being a responsible citizen

Expanding on these three core themes further, the content that covers these is as follows:

- 'Health and wellbeing' looks at physical and emotional health and reminds us that it's important to look at these two areas together and to give weight to both across the curriculum. Using the 'knowledge, skills and understanding' approach with this topic, there should be opportunities for pupils to look at ways of keeping themselves safe and to develop skills in managing their own physical and emotional health.

- 'Relationships' is closely linked to health and wellbeing. It helps children to look beyond themselves and their needs and to consider the different relationships we have in life and how best to manage them, both offline and online.

- 'Living in the wider world – economic wellbeing and being a responsible citizen' pushes the thinking further out: we start with self, then others, and then the wider world. This area also addresses skills for future employment and managing money. We already know that this world is and will be challenging and complex, so this is an essential but often neglected area of PSHE. Within this theme, pupils should have the opportunity to look at and reflect on rights, responsibilities and respect.

They should explore equality and diversity and begin to look at the world of work, money and enterprise.

There are clear areas of overlap between the three areas, but in the simplest terms the themes start with self and move outward to others and then the wider world. All are essential in order to stop PSHE being an exercise just in sitting around talking about feelings. Figure 3.1 shows the relationships between the three core themes.

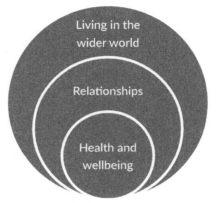

Figure 3.1 The three core themes of PSHE

The three core themes are divided into Key Stage 1 and Key Stage 2, and build on the Early Years Foundation Stage requirements. When planning your scheme of work, it's important that you decide when and in which year you will cover the topics in each Key Stage.

Teaching relationships and sex education

It's the summer term and a rumour flies around the playground: *Today's the day!* There's a nervous buzz in Year Five and Year Six and the teacher closes the blinds in the classroom. The trusty DVD has been dusted off and will perform its conjugal duty once again, just as it has done year in, year out since the mid '90s. Since before some of the staff were even born, perhaps. An hour later the children emerge dazed from the stuffy, darkened classroom and the DVD goes back on the shelf. Sex Ed. duties have been performed for another year.

Hopefully this isn't the extent of the RSE in your school, but in too many this still describes the experience of many pupils. But things are about to change with the introduction of RSE in the *Children and Social*

Work Act 2017.[4] By 2019, all 'pupils of compulsory school age' in all schools must learn about the *relationships* aspect of RSE, and parents may not withdraw their children from this element as they have been able to in the past. The parts of the RSE curriculum that deal with the Science aspects (puberty, reproduction and so on) sit within the National Curriculum for Science, and parents may not withdraw their children from National Curriculum subject areas.

In addition to lessons, schools will be expected to have a policy that is available to parents and others. They must build their RSE curriculum on this basis:

- Safety in forming and maintaining relationships.

- The characteristics of healthy relationships.

- How relationships may affect physical and mental health and wellbeing.

There is an expectation, the wording continues, that this teaching and learning has regard to the age and religious background of the pupils.

In other words, RSE needs primarily to be about relationships – how to form them, keep them and stay safe within them (all relationships) – with due regard to the background of your pupils. There's no need to shy away from teaching all elements of RSE to pupils because of their religious or cultural background, but teachers do need to recognise and be sensitive towards the different experiences of pupils within a range of relationships, both present and future.

With these changes and updates in mind, if your school's teaching sounds like the story at the beginning of the section, now is a good time to revise and revisit your RSE provision.

In planning this book I asked teachers about how they stay up to date with PSHE issues. One responded that they didn't because PSHE doesn't really change. I would argue that PSHE – and RSE as part of that – is in fact the subject that changes the most. A few years ago we didn't have the access to social media that we have now and children weren't engaging in social media at such a young age (despite age restrictions). New forms of social media have emerged, and changes can be fast and confusing.

---

4 *Children and Social Work Act 2017*, Chapter 4. Retrieved 23 January 2018 from www.legislation.gov.uk.

Consent is a big issue, too. With historical sex-abuse cases and sexual-harassment stories emerging across all industries, there's a real need to enable children to stay safe, recognise risk and ask for help. We also need to enable all children to recognise and understand boundaries and what constitutes acceptable behaviour with others.

Consent and social media collide as the ease of taking, swapping and sharing photographs and video (including live video) increases and as children communicate online. A report from the NSPCC[5] found that one in four children has experienced something upsetting online, including unwanted sexual messages.

Clever online algorithms select advertising based on age, interest and internet searches, so that every time we use our computers or other devices we're bombarded with advertising that has been carefully selected just for us. So teaching robust RSE is about keeping children safe, helping them stay informed on issues such as consent, social media and advertising, and ensuring that they are ready for healthy consensual relationships when they are older. It needs to address physical and emotional changes and to help prepare them for changing relationships, both now and in the future.

When we look at the bigger picture then RSE seems less of a chore and more of a necessity, and this shows how a few DVD clips at the end of Key Stage 2 cannot possibly fulfil all of your school's RSE needs. Being able to tell you the changes that happen in puberty, some reproduction basics and maybe how a baby is born is a start, but is it enough? Children may be left with questions like these:

- 'Why did we just learn that? How will that help us in our lives? Do I need to use this learning now or in the future?'

- 'I understand the basics, but I'd like to talk about some questions I have. Who can I go to? I'm not sure my parents will be able to explain the topic to me.'

- 'Are we going to learn some more about this at a later date?'

- 'Will we get a chance to revisit what we've learnt and check our understanding, or is that it?'

---

5 Lilley, C., Ball, R. and Vernon, H. (2014) *The Experiences of 11–16 Year Olds on Social Networking Sites.* London: NSPCC. Accessed at https://www.nspcc.org.uk/globalassets/documents/research-reports/experiences-11-16-year-olds-social-networking-sites-report.pdf on 11 January 2018.

And for the teacher:

- 'Am I confident that the pupils have developed new skills, have discussed their understanding of the topic and are able to apply their knowledge?'

- 'How do I know?'

- 'Are they able to tackle a problem if they come across it in real life?'

- 'Do I need to revisit some of the areas of learning to ensure understanding of the topic?'

- 'Have I presented opportunities for children to practise using their understanding in real-life situations?'

In order to plan and teach meaningful RSE we need a starting point. The list below – from Brook, the PSHE Association and the Sex Education Forum, in their 2014 document *Sex and Relationships Education (SRE) for the 21st Century*[6] – is a good checklist.

SRE is a partnership between home and schools which:

1. ensures children and young people's views are actively sought to influence lesson planning and teaching

2. starts early and is relevant to pupils at each stage in their development and maturity

3. is taught by people who are trained and confident in talking about issues such as healthy and unhealthy relationships, equality, pleasure, respect, abuse, sexuality, gender identity, sex and consent

4. includes the acquisition of knowledge, the development of life skills and respectful attitudes and values

5. has sufficient time to cover a wide range of topics, with a strong emphasis on relationships, consent, rights,

---

6   Brook, PSHE Association and Sex Education Forum (2014) *Sex and Relationships Education (SRE) for the 21st Century.* London: Brook, PSHE Association and Sex Education Forum.

responsibilities to others, negotiation and communication skills, and accessing services

6. helps pupils understand on and offline safety, consent, violence and exploitation

7. is both medically and factually correct and treats sex as a normal and pleasurable fact of life

8. is inclusive of difference: gender identity, sexual orientation, disability, ethnicity, culture, age, faith or belief, or other life experience

9. uses active learning methods, and is rigorously planned, assessed and evaluated

10. helps pupils understand a range of views and beliefs about relationships and sex in society including some of the mixed messages about gender, sex and sexuality from different sources including the media

11. teaches pupils about the law and their rights to confidentiality even if they are under 16, and is linked to school-based and community health services and organisations

12. promotes equality in relationships, recognises and challenges gender inequality and reflects girls' and boys' different experiences and needs.

Let's look at these elements individually so that we can begin to construct meaningful RSE experiences that work across the whole school.

1. 'ensures children and young people's views are actively sought to influence planning and teaching'

Seeking pupils' views can start with the group who have just received their RSE sessions. Ask a small group to come and have a chat with you. (Include a cross-section of pupils.) Ask them some questions and encourage them to be truthful and constructive in their responses. Questions might include:

• What have you learnt this year?/What are you going to learn this year?

- Tell me some of the facts you have learnt in your lessons.

- Tell me some of the skills you have learnt in your lessons.

- What sort of activities did you do (e.g. drama, completing worksheets, watching videos)?

- Which activities helped you learn the best?

- Were there any activities that didn't work for you? If so, why not?

- Were the lessons helpful to you? In what ways?

- Did the school help your parents understand what you were learning and how?

- Did you evaluate your learning in the lessons? Did the teacher ask what you thought of the lesson, what you learned and what you enjoyed?

- How could we make RSE learning even better for other pupils in the school?

- Is there someone you can go to if you have questions or concerns in relation to RSE?

These are just sample questions. Record the children's responses by jotting down their answers. Ensure that what they say is kept confidential. (However, if a child makes a disclosure or if you have concerns, follow your school's safeguarding policy or speak to your Designated Safeguarding Lead.) The answers to these questions can help shape your understanding both of what children have learnt in their sessions and of their understanding.

In association with the National Children's Bureau (NCB), the Sex Education Forum has produced a toolkit, *A Toolkit for Involving Primary School Children in Reviewing Sex and Relationships Education*. This contains a wealth of information and activities based around involving pupils in reviewing and developing your school's programme of RSE.[7]

---

7   Emmerson, L. with Lees, J. (2013) *Let's Get It Right: A Toolkit for Involving Primary School Children in Reviewing Sex and Relationships Education*. London: Sex Education Forum and National Children's Bureau.

2. 'starts early and is relevant to pupils at each stage in their development and maturity'

It's important to introduce RSE as a whole from early on, so that children learn and build on previous knowledge (according to age and ability).

Many aspects of RSE fall within the greater remit of a well-planned PSHE programme. If you're not sure what RSE would look like in Key Stage 1, for example, start with the end outcome – for instance, Year Six pupils learn about changing and growing, including the physical and emotional changes during puberty – and then build backwards. In Year Five you might introduce the basics of puberty and body changes and why these happen. In Year Four you could talk about how our friendships and relationships change and also explore issues of conflict management in the context of growing up and changing. In Year Three, children could be learning about physical and emotional changes they've been through since they were babies, linked to Science, and you could look forward to the future changes. In Year Two you might talk about simple conflict management and skills around keeping safe and asking for help; in Year One about how babies grow and change; and in Early Years about learning to manage new friendships, sharing and being in a school setting. These suggestions are all examples and could spiral off into and include many other topics, such as consent, friendship, conflict management, personal hygiene, families, aspiration, managing risk and where to get help.

As another example with a different starting point, you might want to think about how to introduce the topics of personal safety and consent in straightforward, age-appropriate ways that are echoed throughout the school. The NSPCC has developed some resources[8] for helping children stay safe from sexual abuse which may be helpful for use in work on consent. They include teacher guidance, a lesson plan, a presentation and a leaflet, and the resources have the PSHE Association's Quality Mark.

---

8   NSPCC (n.d.) *PANTS – Resources for Schools and Teachers.* www.nspcc.org.uk/preventing-abuse/keeping-children-safe/underwear-rule/underwear-rule-schools-teaching-resources.

The key message is 'PANTS':

● PANTS ─────────────────────────────────

- **P**rivates are private.

- **A**lways remember your body belongs to you.

- **N**o means no.

- **T**alk about secrets that upset you.

- **S**peak up, someone can help.

---

3. 'is taught by people who are trained and confident in talking about issues such as healthy and unhealthy relationships, equality, pleasure, respect, abuse, sexuality, gender identity, sex and consent'

RSE deals with complex topics, so training and support are an important part. It's essential to have well-trained teachers who have attended up-to-date training from a reputable trainer, such as the PSHE Association, the Sex Education Forum or the Christopher Winter Project. You may have local providers who can help or you could ask the school nurse to recommend someone. Cascade this training to all staff (not just the Key Stage 2 staff).

Stay up to date by reading key documents, including the latest government and Ofsted guidance or advice. RSE is changing rapidly, so aim to stay in touch with any changes to policy. Just by reading this book you've started taking steps in the right direction.

4. 'includes the acquisition of knowledge, the development of life skills and respectful attitudes and values'

Knowledge is a good starting point, but it's also essential that pupils have the opportunity to discuss and explore ideas. What skills do they need now? What skills will they need next term or next year?

If you're introducing the topic of puberty and body changes, the factual knowledge about what happens at puberty is the starting point. Now make sure you explore associated feelings and where children can go for help if they need it, both within and outside of school. Discuss behaviours associated with puberty, such as mood swings, changes in friendships and teasing.

In order to do this effectively you need curriculum time, which is always at a premium. In Chapter Two we looked at ways of delivering PSHE in an over-crowded curriculum. Consider how you allocate pockets of time and how this may affect planning and delivery. This leads on to point five...

5. 'has sufficient time to cover a wide range of topics, with a strong emphasis on relationships, consent, rights, responsibilities to others, negotiation and communication skills, and accessing services'

'Sufficient time' is the bane of everyone's life in school, but it's important to make sure that time dedicated to RSE is allocated and protected. This is where the spiral curriculum comes in. RSE should be taught at age-appropriate levels throughout the child's primary school career: it needn't be crammed into the top of Key Stage 2. For example, as we've already seen, relationships should be taught from Early Years upwards, as should topics like 'keeping myself safe', 'managing conflict' and 'our responsibilities to others'. If these are embedded *throughout* the PSHE programme of study, that reduces the pressure at the top of Key Stage 2.

6. 'helps pupils understand on and offline safety, consent, violence and exploitation'

Again, these topics should be embedded throughout the whole PSHE curriculum and will be covered in other subject areas too. When it comes to RSE in particular, it's important to recap on managing risk, personal safety and where to go for help, and to link this with work on recognising and developing healthy relationships.

7. 'is both medically and factually correct and treats sex as a normal and pleasurable fact of life'

School nurses will describe sexual organs as just another part of the body, like the digestive system, and while teachers are not expected to be health professionals, we can take a leaf out of their book. Always use the correct vocabulary for parts of the body and check your own understanding. (For example, are you using the word 'vagina' when you actually mean 'vulva'?) Acknowledge that there are many different words for the reproductive organs but that in school you will use the correct biological terms. If as a teacher you are unused to saying these words, then prepare and practise. Say the words to yourself until they become as ordinary as 'fraction' or 'adverb'.

Parents sometimes worry that teaching children about sex being a normal occurrence within a consensual adult relationship will encourage them to experiment, but the opposite is true.[9] Abstinence-only and 'Just Say No' programmes are also damaging,[10] so reassure parents that all teaching is age-appropriate and that children are given only the information they need to know for now.

8. 'is inclusive of difference: gender identity, sexual orientation, disability, ethnicity, culture, age, faith or belief, or other life experience'

Teachers sometimes worry that they don't know enough about different faith viewpoints and what stance to take when teaching RSE. Follow the key principles about good practice in PSHE by informing parents, setting ground rules, ensuring that learning is age-appropriate and well planned, and acknowledging that this is only one part of children's learning on sex. Be sensitive to the wide variety of backgrounds, cultures, family experiences and the experiences of your pupils. Recap the section in Chapter One on 'Approaching difference and diversity in PSHE' and remember always that children may have a broad experience of what 'family' means to them.

The key for teaching RSE to children who follow a faith is to be sensitive and inclusive and to acknowledge that some pupils may have an expectation that future healthy partnerships will be in the form of marriage. Similarly, some children will have learnt from their families to expect that any sexual relationship they may have will be within marriage. Whatever future relationships children may have, and whatever form those may take, they will still need to know and understand the principles of what makes a healthy relationship. They also need to be aware of their rights and the laws of the country, and to know where to access support if they need it.

A quick word about female genital mutilation (FGM) and forced marriage. These are not part of religious law but are practised among some cultural groups. Children from certain cultural backgrounds may

---

9   *Review of Key Findings of 'Emerging Answers 2007': Report on Sex Education Programs,* Guttmacher Institute.
10 Guttmacher Institute (2007)

therefore be at risk. If you believe that any of your pupils are at risk of forced marriage or FGM, then it's even more important that they know the law and where they can access support.

FGM is a criminal offence in the UK[11] and is subject to a maximum of 14 years in prison. It is also illegal to take a UK resident overseas for the purpose of FGM. If teachers have information that a girl under the age of 18 has undergone FGM, or if they see any physical signs that a girl has undergone FGM, then teachers must report this to the police. A child at risk may be subject to a protection order and there are close links to safeguarding and child protection.

Similarly, forced marriage is also a criminal offence in the UK under the Anti-Social Crime and Policing Act 2014, and this includes taking somebody overseas to force them to marry. A child who is at risk may experience emotional or physical coercion and (as with FGM) may be subject to a protection order. Some pupils may expect to have an *arranged* marriage, but this should be a free choice and have support from both families: this is different from *forced* marriage, which is an abuse of human rights.

For more information on FGM and forced marriage, look at the key pages on the NSPCC and Childline websites.[12]

9. 'uses active learning methods, and is rigorously planned, assessed and evaluated'

'Active learning' means moving away from the beloved DVD and associated worksheets. By all means use a DVD clip as one resource or as a jumping-off point for further learning, but think creatively about how your pupils learn best, what will help you deliver your objectives and how you will assess learning.

If you're teaching about consent, for instance, you could start with some 'Agree/Disagree' statements, set up some scenarios to explore and solve, discuss potential situations, use 'freeze-frame' to set up a 'What happens next?' scenario, explore different responses and being assertive...and so on.

Build assessment opportunities into the activities (see the section 'Introducing assessment' in Chapter Four), and at the end of a module

---

11 Serious Crime Act 2015 (amendment) www.legislation.gov.uk.

12 See www.nspcc.org.uk/preventing-abuse/child-abuse-and-neglect/female-genital-mutilation-fgm and www.childline.org.uk/info-advice/bullying-abuse-safety/abuse-safety/female-circumcision-fgm-cutting.

use a more formal method of assessment to check whether you're meeting your success criteria and whether there are any gaps in knowledge or understanding. After the module, run a focus group or survey to evaluate what worked and what could be done better.

10. 'helps pupils understand a range of views and beliefs about relationships and sex in society including some of the mixed messages about gender, sex and sexuality from different sources including the media'

There is hardly ever one simple answer or viewpoint when it comes to RSE, so be sensitive to the fact that others will have a variety of views. Explore different viewpoints (a 'conscience corridor' may help with this: this is explained in the section 'Using drama techniques' in Chapter Four) and the fact children may come across mixed messages in the media. Remind them that if they have any concerns or questions it's okay to ask for help.

11. 'teaches pupils about the law and their rights to confidentiality even if they are under 16, and is linked to school-based and community health services and organisations'

By setting clear ground rules together you'll already have explained confidentiality and how and where to ask for help. Check the latest laws regarding elements of RSE, including laws relevant to sharing explicit media, sexual consent and staying safe. Stay up to date by checking the Sex Education Forum website.

12. 'promotes equality in relationships, recognises and challenges gender inequality and reflects girls' and boys' different experiences and needs'

The key word here is 'promotes'. It's essential that we address the fact that families and relationships can be widely diverse. Talk about and discuss the fact that we may see the world in different ways but that we need to respect others' choices, even if they are not the same as our own. Teasing and bullying in any form needs to be tackled. Don't shy away from discussing difference and gender-stereotyping and remind children that it's okay to have differences of opinion.

The *Toolkit* produced by the Sex Education Forum and the National Children's Bureau reminds us which topics are appropriate for which ages:[13]

- Ages 3–6: the difference between girls and boys, naming body parts, where babies come from, friends and family, what areas of the body are private, and who they can talk to if they are worried.

- Ages 7–8: changing nature of friendship, emotional and physical changes of growing up, similarities and differences between girls and boys, coping with strong emotions, how babies are made from eggs and sperm, how to look after our bodies, and how to be safe and healthy.

- Ages 9–10: love and different types of families, puberty and sexual feelings, changing body image, conception, how babies develop and are born and why families are important for having babies, how people can get diseases, including HIV from sex, and prevent them, and who to talk to if they want help or advice, as well as information on puberty and sex.

In 2009 a wide range of key stakeholders and experts across London created a document for Young London Matters called *SRE Core Curriculum for London: A Practical Resource*,[14] and this contained a suggested primary curriculum overview that takes into account all of the advice and good practice above. Based on the spiral curriculum, it builds on knowledge, skills and understanding year by year to provide a comprehensive programme. You'll notice the broad range of topics which cover many other parts of the PSHE curriculum, too, so if you're in the process of reviewing or redeveloping your own curriculum, this may serve as a starting point.

---

13 Adapted from Emmerson, L. with Lees, J. (2013) *Let's Get It Right: A Toolkit for Involving Primary School Children in Reviewing Sex and Relationships Education.* London: Sex Education Forum and National Children's Bureau.

14 Young London Matters (2009) *SRE Core Curriculum for London: A Practical Resource.* London: Government Office for London.

Table 3.1 Suggested topics for primary school's scheme of work on RSE

Foundation Stage	Key Stage 1			Key Stage 2			
Early Years	Year One	Year Two	Year Three	Year Four	Year Five	Year Six
˙Myself and others	˙Myself and others	Differences: boys and girls	˙Self-esteem	˙Changing and growing	Talking about puberty	Puberty and reproduction
˙Family networks	˙Body parts	Differences: male and female	Challenging gender stereotypes	Body changes and reproduction	Becoming men and women	Relationships and reproduction
˙Body awareness	˙Family	Naming body parts	Differences: male and female	What is puberty?	Puberty and hygiene	Conception and puberty
˙Hygiene	˙Friendships	*Everybody needs caring for	Family differences	˙Thinking, feeling, doing – changing relationships	Menstruation and wet dreams	Being a parent
	˙Choices	˙Looking after the body	˙Decision-making	˙Assertiveness	Menstruation education for girls	HIV transmission
			˙Safety	Your questions answered	˙Building good relationships	Your questions answered

* Topics marked with an asterisk have a close correlation with the drug-education life-skills approach that we'll look at next.

Young London Matters (2009) SRE Core Curriculum for London: A Practical Resource. London: Government Office for London

You'll know your pupils and your school best, and once you've fully reviewed your RSE provision you'll have a good ideas of which topics you'll want to teach and when. The bottom line is this: if we are to equip our children for the challenges of the future and to enable them to have healthy, mutually supportive relationships, then we need to address all aspects of RSE.

● CASE STUDY ───────────────

I always really enjoy teaching RSE to kids. It is usually done in a very scientific way and I think adults, especially the parents, perhaps worry too much about the outcome as they obviously have a lot more knowledge and life experience and they feel concerned about how the lessons will affect their kids. But children and adults look at it very differently, thankfully! On the whole to the kids it's just another lesson but more exciting because we have to close the door and the parents need to see the teachers for a meeting before the lesson starts. As times are changing so fast and relationships get more and more complicated, a solid RSE curriculum is more important than ever and school may be the only place where kids can safely ask questions or say words like 'vagina' and 'penis' over and over without getting into trouble!

PSHE teacher

Teaching about drugs and alcohol

While the prevalence of young people drinking alcohol and taking drugs continues on a downward trend,[15] there is still a need to address drug and alcohol education in school and to help children and young people assess the risks.

The Alcohol and Drug Education and Prevention Information Service (ADEPIS), established in 2013 by the prevention charity Mentor UK, is the leading source for schools of evidence-based information and tools for alcohol and drug education and prevention. Mentor-ADEPIS defines a drug as a 'substance people take to change the way they feel, think or behave'.[16] This definition includes legal and illegal drugs, including medicines, new psychoactive substances (which used to be known as 'legal highs'), tobacco and tobacco substitutes, and alcohol.

A little like the RSE curriculum, drug education has traditionally focused on delivering facts and information, but a well-planned holistic approach to developing skills and exploring attitudes, values and understanding makes for better long-term education. In its 2015 study of schools' provision, Mentor-ADEPIS[17] found barriers to effective drug education similar to those affecting other aspects of PSHE: the constraints of curriculum time, a lack of resources

---

15 Statistics Team, NHS Digital (2017) *Smoking, Drinking and Drug Use among Young People.* London: NHS Digital.

16 http://mentor-adepis.org/frequently-asked-questions.

17 Thurman, B. and Boughelaf, J. (2015) *'We Don't Get Taught Enough': An Assessment of Drug Education Provision in Schools in England.* London: Mentor-ADEPIS.

and the fact that teachers were non-specialists. Research conducted by the PSHE Association on behalf of Mentor-ADEPIS[18] found that primary-age pupils receive between one and two hours of drug and alcohol education per school year. So perhaps we need to start looking at what works in drug education and identifying the overlaps with other PSHE areas and how drug education fits into the spiral curriculum, so that we don't end up with just one or two bolted-on 'Drugs: the facts' sessions somewhere in Key Stage 2.

Mentor-ADEPIS recommends that good drug education should:

- be needs-led and age-appropriate, putting the pupil at the centre

- be a two-way, interactive process of learning

- enable pupils to explore their own and other people's attitudes and values

- challenge misconceptions about the prevalence and acceptability of drug use among peers

- develop pupils' personal and social skills to manage risk, solve problems and communicate effectively.[19]

Using a life-skills approach, Mentor-ADEPIS suggests that children should learn about 'assertiveness and managing social situations, making and keeping positive friendships and considering attitudes, values and decision-making'.[20] In other words, drug education works best as part of a whole programme of well-planned PSHE which meets children's needs and includes active and engaging lessons that help develop social skills and give space for reflection. This should sound pretty familiar by now. While learning information about alcohol and drugs (both legal and illegal) is part of this, the best way to help children to develop their resilience and be better able to manage the risks associated with drugs and alcohol is through practising related skills.

---

18 Boddington, N., McWhirter, J. and Stonehouse, A. (2013) *Drug and Alcohol Education in Schools.* London: PSHE Association and Mentor-ADEPIS.

19 Thurman, B. and Boughelaf, J. (2015) *'We Don't Get Taught Enough': An Assessment of Drug Education Provision in Schools in England.* London: Mentor-ADEPIS.

20 Mentor-ADEPIS (2016) *Life-Skills Based Education for Alcohol and Drug Prevention: Alcohol and Drug Prevention Briefing Paper.* London: Mentor-ADEPIS.

With this in mind, what should drug and alcohol education look like in schools? Think of the spiral curriculum that runs from the Early Years up to the top of Key Stage 2. At Foundation Stage, as part of 'Personal social and emotional development', children learn about basic hygiene and keeping themselves safe. They might experience the home corner as a doctor's or vet's surgery and develop their play and talking around giving pretend medicines to sick toys. In Key Stage 1 this may develop into some further learning on hygiene and keeping themselves clean and healthy, perhaps linked to Science. Children will learn about different medicines that they might take occasionally when they're ill (such as antibiotics) and medicines that help prevent disease (such as vaccinations). They learn about people who help keep them healthy and about safety measures around drugs, including the principle that only adults should administer medicines. All the while, the broader PSHE curriculum is based around the common threads of managing risk, developing resilience and communicating. In Key Stage 2, children might learn about smoking and alcohol through Science, and explore the laws that exist to keep them and others safe. Rights and responsibilities in conjunction with the law may come in, as may attitudes towards the media. As part of talking about growing and changing, you might explore the differences between babies, children, teenagers and adults, as well as changing relationships and peer pressure. Managing risk, where to access help and being assertive all come into the programme too, in order to build a scaffold of managing challenges and thriving.

If we look back at Table 3.1, the close correlation between topics that are found in both RSE and drug and alcohol education are clear when taking a life-skills approach. When teaching about risk, you can include examples of scenarios and problem-solving activities that address attitudes towards drugs and education, and which also reinforce and practise general risk-taking skills. For example, you might ask children to consider the following scenarios, to rate the risk as 'Very risky', 'Risky', 'Not very risky' or 'Not at all risky', and then to discuss their answers:

- Trying your friend's asthma inhaler. (*We should never try anyone else's medicines. They are prescribed for the named person only.*)

- Taking a headache tablet without asking an adult. (*Always ask an adult, even if you've taken that medicine before.*)

- Washing your hands with plain water. (*It's better to wash your hands with soap and water.*)

- Taking a sip of your parent's beer or wine. (*Under British law, children are legally allowed to taste alcohol in the home from the age of 5. UK chief medical officers recommend, however, that an alcohol-free childhood is the healthiest and best option.*)[21]

- Drinking energy drinks. (*A can of energy drink may have as much caffeine as a cup of espresso or a mug of instant coffee and energy shots often contain more, so the Food Standards Agency recommends they 'should only be consumed in moderation'.*[22] *Such drinks also contain a lot of sugar.*)

You could also invite the children to practise assertiveness skills. For example:

- Your friend's teenage sister offers you some beer and says you have to drink it if you want to be friends with her and her friends. What might you say or do?

- The person sitting next to you at the bus stop keeps blowing cigarette smoke in your direction. What might you say or do?

- Your throat feels sore and your friend offers you a throat sweet. What might you say or do?

Using the 'conscience corridor' activity, you could explore both sides of the smoking argument. One set of pupils could discuss the possible reasons why people smoke, and the other set could discuss the reasons why it's best not to smoke. As a child or an adult passes through the corridor, they hear both sides of the argument ('Cigarettes cost a lot of money', 'Smoking makes you look cool', 'Smoking makes your breath smell', 'It's fun smoking with your friends', etc.). You could then discuss the pros and cons, the risks, and relevant laws and responsibilities.

Drug and alcohol education may benefit from visits and visitors, but consider carefully before booking any visitors – how will they fit into your planned programme of drug education and PSHE as a whole? For advice on this, read the section in Chapter Five on 'Making

---

21 Donaldson, Sir L., Chief Medical Officer for England (2009) *Guidance on the Consumption of Alcohol by Children and Young People.* London: Department of Health.

22 www.food.gov.uk/science/additives/energydrinks.

visits and inviting visitors'. Mentor-ADEPIS has found that talks from former addicts, although they may be compelling and exciting, may not have long-term benefits to pupils and certainly shouldn't replace well-planned drug-education lessons in school. If you have access to a school nurse, a health professional or a pharmacist, they may be able to help with sessions on hand-washing, hygiene and medicines; Theatre in Education companies may offer a show and a workshop that addresses drug education; and community police officers may be able to help with the law around drugs and alcohol. As always with PSHE, though, ensure that any content is part of your planned programme of PSHE, and also that *all* aspects are covered – not just the 'Don'ts'. While it's tempting to hand over tricky topics to specialists, these topics are only part of the programme. Always check the background and qualifications of providers; if you're ever unsure, contact Mentor-ADEPIS or the PSHE Association for advice.

As with RSE, school is only *part* of the jigsaw, so it's important that parents and carers understand how you intend to teach about drugs and alcohol and what they can do to support this at home. Having a clear policy will help with this. Unlike other policies, however, the drug policy is not just about how and what you intend to teach: it should also contain a section in which you outline how you will deal with drug-related incidents. This includes the steps you plan to take if a pupil is found with drugs or medicines in school, your school's stance around alcohol on the premises (including staff parties and fundraisers), how any alcohol on the premises will be kept away from children, and the steps you would take if you suspected that a parent or carer was intoxicated while looking after a child. Mentor-ADEPIS has a policy toolkit that will help when reviewing or rewriting your school's policy.[23]

● CASE STUDY

Our school was approached by a drug education charity offering to come in and talk to our children about drugs. We didn't feel particularly confident about our drug education (in fact we had let it slip for a while), so we jumped at the chance. I looked at

---

23 Mentor-ADEPIS (2012) *Reviewing Your Drug and Alcohol Policy: A Toolkit for Schools.* London: Mentor-ADEPIS.

their website before the visit and felt a bit worried about some of the messages. It seemed a bit scary for our children, so I emailed the contact person and asked if they wouldn't mind sending over their lesson plans so I could check them out before the visit. I didn't get a reply, so I tried digging a little further on their website and found that the charity is funded by the Church of Scientology. I felt a bit annoyed that they hadn't been up front with us and cancelled the visit, as it wasn't for us. I'm not sure the parents would have been too impressed either!

Deputy head

✪ SOMETHING TO THINK ABOUT

Review your drug and alcohol provision alongside RSE, and check that this is a spiral curriculum. Are there any overlaps or gaps? How do the two topics support each other? Check your policies to ensure that they are up to date and that they address the needs of your school.

The following have the best up-to-date information on RSE:

- *Sex Education Forum*: Provides up-to-date information, resources and support for all aspects of RSE (www. sexeducationforum.org.uk).

- *PSHE Association*: Offers advice on teaching and learning in all aspects of PSHE, including RSE (www.pshe-association.org.uk).

- *Brook*: Provides sexual health advice for young people and offers training and support to anyone teaching RSE (www.brook.org.uk).

The following have the best up-to-date information on drug and alcohol education:

- *Mentor-ADEPIS*: Provides resources, advice, training and seminars across the country (http://mentor-adepis.org).

- *Hope UK*: Provides drug education for children, parents and youth workers (www.hopeuk.org).

- *Drug Wise:* Promotes evidence-based information on drugs, alcohol and tobacco (www.drugwise.org.uk).

- *Talk to Frank:* The government portal on drug education for young people, this gives the latest up-to-date information on drugs (www.talktofrank.com).

- *Department for Education and the Association of Chief Police Officers (ACPO):* Provides drug advice for schools (www.gov.uk/government/publications/drugs-advice-for-schools).

- *Alcohol Education Trust:* Offers support for teachers and parents on young people and drinking (http:// alcoholeducationtrust.org).

- *Drink Aware:* Works to reduce alcohol misuse and harm in the UK (www.drinkaware.co.uk).

- *Christopher Winter Project:* Promotes the teaching of drug and alcohol education with confidence and the teaching of RSE with confidence in primary schools – resource packs and training (http://cwpresources.co.uk).

Teaching about change, loss and bereavement

As a teacher, this is another topic that may make you feel more vulnerable, but it is an important part of the PSHE curriculum. Everyone experiences change all the time, from small changes like having a haircut to huge changes like changing school, home or country. Loss may come in the form of broken friendships or family breakdown or be part of the grief process. Giving children the skills to tackle change and to manage their feelings will help them begin to approach life's greater challenges with the best emotional tools.

According to research, up to 70 per cent of schools have a bereaved pupil on roll at any given time, and 92 per cent of young people will experience a significant bereavement before the age of 16.[24] While every child deals with loss in a different way and needs support at and

---

24 Harrison, L. and Harrington, R. (2001) 'Adolescents' bereavement experiences: Prevalence, association with depressive symptoms, and use of services.' *Journal of Adolescence 24,* 2, 159–169.

beyond class level, establishing a safe learning ethos ensures pupils are able to express their feelings.

The PSHE Association's *Programme of Study*[25] suggests that through Core Theme One, 'Health and wellbeing', pupils should have the opportunity to learn:

- At Key Stage 1: about change and loss and the associated feelings (including moving home, and losing toys, pets or friends)

- At Key Stage 2: about change, including transitions (between Key Stages and schools), loss, separation, divorce and bereavement.

Talking about loss and change can be tricky as we've all experienced some form of loss and it can make us feel vulnerable. Protecting your own emotional health and wellbeing is key, so before talking about loss in class, reflect on your own feelings, how you manage them and where your own vulnerabilities lie. Use ground rules to set clear boundaries. Distancing can also be a useful technique here, such that discussions focus around imaginary scenarios, characters in books or puppets.

Possible activities for Key Stage 1 include looking at how the children have changed and will change in their lives: what they looked like as babies and toddlers and what they could and couldn't do. You could talk about starting school and how they've changed from then to now and what changes they might see as they go into Key Stage 2 and beyond (e.g. reading harder books, starting a new hobby, a faith-based rite of passage, getting taller). You could make personal or class timelines and talk about the feelings children may experience along these steps. You could use a character or puppet who is about to experience a change like starting school or moving home and ask pupils to offer the character some advice. You could create a change toolkit for the character and ask pupils to draw what they would put in it (e.g. a cuddle from a friend, a deep breath, a chat with the character's parent or drawing a picture of things that make us happy).

---

25 PSHE Association (2017) *Programme of Study*. London: PSHE Association.

In moving on to talking about bereavement and greater loss in Key Stage 1, build on this learning about change and take gentle steps. Child Bereavement UK suggests that children between the ages of five and eight recognise that dead people are different from those who are alive, and by about seven years old most accept that death is inevitable and will eventually happen to everyone. However, children may hide their feelings and appear outwardly fine, so it is important to provide time and support to ensure that their questions are answered. At this age they may also be interested in rituals surrounding death, so there are close links with Religious Education. Any learning should of course be sensitive to the different experiences of pupils, depending on their family, culture and faith. Picture books can provide a useful starting point in beginning discussion about feelings associated with loss and can help reassure children that if they are worried they can talk to someone about their feelings.

In Key Stage 2, children will often have feelings of anxiety about going to secondary school, so being able to openly discuss any worries and concerns they have is a key part of managing that transition. Fears may include the challenges of making new friends, independent travel, a bigger workload and being around older pupils. While Year Six pupils will have the chance to visit secondary and senior schools, consider setting up an opportunity for older pupils to come and talk to younger pupils about what to expect, or set up an activity day where older and younger pupils work together on a project or a challenge. If you have a local Junior Citizens scheme, pupils can be given the chance to look at the skills involved in independent travel and, of course, this will reinforce previous learning on managing risk and staying safe.

Older pupils may already have experienced loss and bereavement, and talking about managing a range of feelings will give them a broader sense of managing loss as part of life. Child Bereavement UK notes that children at Key Stage 2 recognise that death is irreversible, and although they may struggle still with abstract concepts, they understand the link with their own mortality. This may lead to insecurity or anxiety, so it's important that they know there are people who can support them if they have concerns.

If your school doesn't already have a bereavement policy, it's worth creating one so that everyone knows the steps the school will take in the event of the loss of any member of the school community. While this may seem morbid, it's perhaps helpful to be prepared, in the same way that we prepare for fire by having extinguishers and practising fire drills.

Divorce and changes in family circumstances can also deeply affect children, and they may experience feelings of grief if a parent leaves the home or if family circumstances change. It's also crucial to be sensitive to the needs of a child who may be experiencing ongoing family conflict. Offer a listening ear and allow children to express themselves. Ensure that any transitions are as smooth as possible by making sure the school administration is informed and up to date. When teaching about families, be sensitive on celebration days like Mother's Day and Father's Day.

A child's first experience of bereavement might be the loss of a pet, and it's important to take this seriously and to ensure that the child has the time and space to talk about their feelings. Sometimes the simplest form of support is what's needed – a listening ear, some private time in the classroom at playtime, and pens and paper to draw a picture of the lost pet and recall their happy memories.

Talking about loss, change and bereavement shouldn't be all doom and gloom, however. Helping children prepare mentally and emotionally for change can take away the sting of anxiety, and it's good to explore the positive side of changes too, rather than dwelling only on the negative. Try activities like a 'conscience corridor' to get children thinking about the pros and cons of a change like moving school ('It's scary…but it means you're growing up', 'You'll have to take the bus…but you get to hang out with your friends on the way to school', and so on).

Some tried-and-tested activities around change, loss and bereavement include these:

- *Natural objects.* Create a set of natural objects that have changed: pressed leaves, seeds, shells, fossils, twigs. Ask the children to identify the objects in groups and to talk about how they might be used. Have the objects always been like this? What did they look like before they changed? Has their purpose changed? (For example, a shell used to have a mollusc living in it but is now decorative; a star anise used to be the fruit of a tree but can now be used as a cooking ingredient; a leaf used to be part of a tree but can now be composted to nourish new growth.) Everyone and everything in the natural world changes over time, but this doesn't mean that it's not useful or beautiful any more. When someone we love dies we can still look at photographs of them and remember them. We can also create a memory box of pictures and items that help us to remember that person.

- *Paper chain.* Give children strips of paper and pens and ask them to draw and decorate the paper with a change or loss they know about. This may be changing school, losing a pet, a story they've heard or read, or an event they've heard of. Collect the strips together and, in front of the children, glue or staple them together to form a paper chain. This shows how all our experiences of loss and change are interlinked and that everyone experiences them. This activity can be used to express a worry about loss or change or a suggestion on how to manage change, and the paper chain can be a visual stimulus for further discussion.

- *First-aid kit.* Create a class first-aid kit for bereavement, loss or change. Think of things that may help us, including emotional and physical support and knowing where to go to for help. Draw, write or make items to go into the first-aid kit (e.g. a list of people to talk to in school and at home; a safe space for when you're feeling sad; a special toy to cuddle; going for a walk with a family member; a favourite photo). Remind pupils that everyone has different needs and that what works for someone else may not work for them. What helps *them* feel calm and safe?

- *Body outline.* Create a body outline by drawing around someone on large sheets of paper (or use smaller photocopied body outlines). Ask children to write 'feelings words' for change and loss inside the body. Outside the body outline, draw and write ways to support and comfort that person.

- *Music.* Listen to music and talk about the feelings it evokes. Listen to a range of sad music, such as the 'Lacrimosa' from Mozart's *Requiem*, Barber's *Adagio for Strings* or a contemporary song. What is the composer trying to say about their feelings? How does the music tell a story? Are there any parts where the music lifts and sounds hopeful? What might that signify? Then listen to an upbeat piece of music and compare the two. Talk about how music can help us focus and reflect on our feelings.

- *Books.* Create a library of books that allow children to read about loss and reflect on how characters deal with it. Some texts used for English – like *War Horse* and *Private Peaceful*, both by Michael Morpurgo, and E.B. White's *Charlotte's Web* – deal with bereavement and loss. For younger children, picture books like *Goodbye Mog*, by Judith Kerr, and *The Grandad Tree*, written by Trish Cooke and illustrated by Sharon Wilson, can act as a good starting point. Michael Rosen's *Sad Book* and Allan Ahlberg's *My Brother's Ghost* are each based on personal experiences of bereavement.

In Chapter One we talked about values and reflecting on where our values and feelings come from. In preparation for talking about loss, change and bereavement, it's important that you take time to reflect on your own experiences and how these may affect your teaching. Discussions may bring up uncomfortable or vulnerable feelings, so it's important that you are emotionally prepared for this. If you feel okay with it, you may want to remind the children that *everyone* has sad feelings around loss and bereavement, and that includes teachers too. It's okay to feel sad, and you yourself might need to tap into your emotional first-aid kit and take a moment in the lesson, but if you do you'll tell them what's happening.

❋ SOMETHING TO THINK ABOUT

Have a look at your PSHE planning and see where talking about change, loss and bereavement may come in. Perhaps you can link to the text you're looking at in English or to an RE topic on rituals. Consider your own experiences of loss and what you need to put into your own first-aid kit in order to teach this topic.

There are several organisations that provide information, lesson-planning and support for pupils experiencing loss:

- *Child Bereavement UK* – including Elephant's Tea Party, which is part of Child Bereavement UK and provides a way of celebrating life – offers a lot of support for children, parents and families on their website, as well as resources to help teach about bereavement.

- *Cruse Bereavement Care* runs training courses for teachers working with children and young people.

- The *Winston's Wish* charity helps families and children who are experiencing bereavement and offers support for school in the form of information for teachers and a really helpful schools pack.

- The *Bereavement Advice Centre* has a free helpline for anyone dealing with bereavement and offers support on all aspects of bereavement and death. It might be worth putting the Centre's number and information on the staffroom noticeboard.

Living in the wider world – economic wellbeing and being a responsible citizen

In the busy PSHE curriculum these areas can end up being a little neglected. The PSHE Association couples the above topics as one Core Theme, but if we split it into two it's easier to see where each fits.

Economic wellbeing

Economic wellbeing covers personal finance, the world of work and employability skills. While it may seem a bit cynical to prepare primary-aged children for the world of work, this entails thinking about the future in the broadest sense, rather than getting them thinking about personal branding like mini *Apprentice* candidates. The world of work and finance for these children will have a different feel to the world of work as we know it. The children we teach are likely to have more than one job and more than one career, and may experience employment or go straight to the world of self-employment or owning a business. Job titles and roles may be harder to pin down. Their work will be dictated by changes to technology and by greater diversity and greater flexibility within the job market. A global survey commissioned by

Polycom[26] in 2017 found that two-thirds of the world's workforce took advantage of 'anywhere working' (from home, working remotely rather than being in one set workplace) as opposed to 12 per cent in May 2012 – a rapid shift in just a few years. The numbers are much higher for millennials than for the 45–60 age group and may indicate a pattern for children who will be entering the workforce in the future.

Given the rapidly changing nature of work, it's the skills associated with working that children need to start developing: self-motivation, independence, creativity, resilience, managing relationships that may be real or virtual, developing working relationships quickly and effectively, personal management, and so on. Many of these skills will be taught and practised in various subject areas, but again PSHE can be the delivery vehicle for these skills too, using the common threads.

It's important to make the learning relevant to the age of your pupils so that they see the connections between their own lives now and their future lives. Talk about different routes through learning, including university, apprenticeships, work and qualifications, so that children understand that there is a range of options. Talk about *what they might like to do* when they're older, but also about *who they might like to be* and *what they will contribute to the world* – help pupils to see that they are part of a community and a member of society, and that they have a contribution to make. Encourage them to reflect on those who contribute to the school community, the local community and the wider global community.

The world of money is also changing quickly as money becomes more virtual. Again, in the last few years contactless and mobile payments have become the norm rather than the exception, and it can be easy to lose track of spending when it's just numbers on a screen. While children will learn about money in Maths, this can easily be linked to managing money with a PSHE slant. The organisation Young Money has a vision of a society, 'in which all children and young people have the skills, knowledge and confidence to manage their money well, now and in the future'. It's good to note that close link to PSHE, with the mention of skills as well as knowledge.

---

26 Polycom (2017) *The Changing World of Work: Digital Whitepaper.* Polycom, Inc. Accessed at www.polycom.co.uk/content/dam/polycom/common/documents/whitepapers/ changing-needs-of-the-workplace-whitepaper-enus.pdf on 11 January 2018.

One of the most relevant ways of teaching about money and the value of money is in giving children real-world problems to solve. Situations like planning a party, running a charity event or fundraiser, buying new equipment for the classroom or playground or running a book fair can offer opportunities for children of every age to participate in real-life events. Imagine that you're planning a disco for the end of term. As a class, decide what things you need for your disco and perhaps plan a theme. Give pupils a budget and an aim – perhaps to cover the initial outlay or to make money for charity. Split the class into groups and set each a task: decorating, allocating roles, preparing snacks and deciding whether to charge for snacks, choosing music, deciding on an entry fee, providing entertainment, and so on. As the teacher you can guide the groups, but part of the learning is theorising and working out problems. If the group decides that the entry fee should be higher than usual, get them to debate the pros and cons of this and work out costs. They could compare prices of bulk-buying snacks and drinks and buying generic or branded goods.

Younger children too can access real-life problems at their own level of learning, not just the older children. Plan the class stall for a school fair or jumble sale and get pupils pricing goods and managing the float. Afterwards, get them to count the money and work out any profit.

Try imaginary scenarios too. You could link budgeting to RSE and ask children to think of the equipment a baby needs and then use baby-equipment websites to work out how much it will cost. If a newborn baby goes through eight nappies a day, how many nappies is that per week and how much would they cost? Young Money has a wide range of resources and information on its website, including video tutorials. Young Money also runs a 'My Money' week in June every year, which could serve as a focus for financial education.

Being a responsible citizen

PSHE, of course, is not all about the self. We need to teach pupils about their place in the world, linked to their rights and responsibilities. It's helpful for children to understand from the youngest age that they are part of a community that starts with them and their family at the centre. They may belong to groups in their community, such as faith groups or hobby, interest and sports groups, but they are also part of the wider community in which they live, and this in turn is part of the UK and the global community. Encourage pupils to think about their role within each community and how they could be active citizens.

School is one community they are part of: how do we show that we belong? What binds us together as members of this community and how do we express that both in and out of school? Talk to the children about difference and diversity, and look at the commonalities between different groups of people rather than the immediately obvious differences.

Looking after the local environment is also part of this, so link to Geography and Science to ensure that pupils understand their responsibility to keep the school grounds and local area tidy and litter-free. You may already organise 'Walk to school' schemes and road-safety training, but link these to the personal aspects. Why is it important for the whole community to think about air quality and pollution in the local area? Who may be affected by dropped litter? (Local wildlife as well as people.) How do we help the less advantaged members of our community, such as the elderly?

Being a responsible citizen links very closely to SMSC, so it may also be addressed in relation to wider school issues and through assemblies. What messages does your school give about being a responsible citizen? Are these messages consistent across the school? How do you communicate these messages to families?

The thread of 'thriving' comes into play here. We want pupils to thrive in their community and to be active members who contribute to society as a whole, and this includes looking at diversity in the broadest sense. Invite local community members to contribute to PSHE lessons to give pupils an understanding of how community is like a huge jigsaw of pieces. Make links with local groups, including those who provide for the elderly and disabled, those involved in the local democratic process (councillors, your local MP, council officers), local shops and providers, and charities and businesses.

Consider becoming a UNICEF 'Rights Respecting School'. Many schools use the Rights Respecting Schools Award as the backbone of their PSHE programme, but remember that although it contributes to many elements of the PSHE curriculum, it doesn't cover everything. You'll still need to map PSHE provision carefully and make sure you cover any topics that don't come under the scheme.

Thinking about mental health

> ...a state of well-being in which every individual realizes his or her own potential, can cope with the normal stresses of life, can work productively and fruitfully, and is able to make a contribution to her or his community.[27]

The above definition from the World Health Organization suggests that good mental health is not simply the absence of illness but the ability to thrive. Teachers are not health professionals or psychotherapists, but we do have a role to play in promoting and supporting positive mental health, as well as in referring those with deeper needs to the appropriate sources of support. Many teachers worry that they'll do more harm than good, and new teachers in particular express concerns that they don't have the skills to deal with mental health problems.

Teachers have a crucial role, however, because they see children on a daily basis and may be able to spot changes in behaviour, attendance or attainment. While these changes may be due to various factors, they might also be indicative of a developing mental health problem. Carefully planned and sensitively taught PSHE can provide the forum in which children can express their worries and where the teacher can pick up on any concerns and signpost the child to further support. If a child makes a disclosure to you during or because of a PSHE lesson, then you can start to put in place the support the child needs. Always refer to your school's safeguarding policy and speak to your Designated Safeguarding Lead (DSL) if you have any concerns.

Pupils who exhibit mental health concerns may be going through extreme stress (due perhaps to social anxiety, pressure to succeed or school phobia) or traumatic experiences (due perhaps to domestic violence or a chaotic home life due to parental drug or alcohol abuse), or they may be experiencing bereavement (including death, a major life change or some other loss).

It's worth being aware of the risk and protective factors for mental health. Table 3.2 is reproduced from guidance supplied by the Department for Education.

---

27 World Health Organization (2014) *Mental Health: A State of Well-Being.* Geneva: World Health Organization.

Table 3.2 Risk and protective factors for mental health

	Risk factors	Protective factors
In the child	• Genetic influences • Low IQ and learning disabilities • Specific development delay or neuro-diversity • Communication difficulties • Difficult temperament • Physical illness • Academic failure • Low self-esteem	• Being female (in younger children) • Secure attachment experience • Outgoing temperament as an infant • Good communication skills, sociability • Being a planner and having a belief in control • Humour • Problem-solving skills and a positive attitude • Experiences of success and achievement • Faith or spirituality • Capacity to reflect
In the family	• Overt parental conflict including domestic violence • Family breakdown (including where children are taken into care or adopted) • Inconsistent or unclear discipline • Hostile or rejecting relationships • Failure to adapt to a child's changing needs • Physical, sexual or emotional abuse • Parental psychiatric illness • Parental criminality, alcoholism or personality disorder • Death and loss – including loss of friendship	• At least one good parent–child relationship (or one supportive adult) • Affection • Clear, consistent discipline • Support for education • Supportive long-term relationship or the absence of severe discord

In the school	• Bullying • Discrimination • Breakdown in or lack of positive friendships • Deviant peer influences • Peer pressure • Poor pupil to teacher relationships	• Clear policies on behaviour and bullying • 'Open-door' policy for children to raise problems • A whole-school approach to promoting good mental health • Positive classroom management • A sense of belonging • Positive peer influences
In the community	• Socio-economic disadvantage • Homelessness • Disaster, accidents, war or other overwhelming events • Discrimination • Other significant life events	• Wider supportive network • Good housing • High standard of living • High morale school with positive policies for behaviour, attitudes and anti-bullying • Opportunities for valued social roles • Range of sport/leisure activities

Department for Education (2015) Mental Health and Behaviour in Schools. London: Department for Education

While it's important for schools to look at the wellbeing of the whole child, there are also implications for the way in which we teach PSHE and the importance of looking at the protective factors. Factors like 'Problem-solving skills and a positive attitude' and 'Capacity to reflect' can be developed through well-planned PSHE sessions, and sessions can also explore and tackle risk factors such as bullying and discrimination. The 'skills' threads running through PSHE also weave through the protective factors here.

The key to teaching and learning about mental health in primary school, therefore, is to help children develop emotional literacy around recognising and naming their own feelings, learning how they can manage these on their own, and knowing when to ask for help. It's another reason, should we need one, why helping children develop skills around managing their own emotional wellbeing is crucial in PSHE. Teachers are well placed to spot any problems and can work with colleagues, parents and agencies like CAMHS (Child and Adolescent Mental Health Services) to support primary-age children in a holistic way.

Learning to be happy?

As part of teaching children to thrive, can we actually teach them to be happy? Should we teach happiness? Isn't a bit of suffering and doom and gloom a natural part of being human?

Independent school Wellington College hit the headlines when they announced they would be teaching a programme of happiness in response to the needs of their pupils. Over a decade later, the programme is still going strong. On closer inspection, however, the programme offered at Wellington is not just about happiness but about lifelong learning, positive mental health and enabling pupils to develop the skills to manage life's challenges. In other words, it matches the aspirations of high-quality, well-planned and taught PSHE. The programme at Wellington is fully embedded within the fabric of the school and has support from the whole community of pupils, staff and parents. The school teaches mindfulness and encourages both pupils and staff to practise this, and it offers a holistic approach to health and wellbeing.

In order to look deeper at happiness, it's worth thinking about what happiness is and why it may need to be part of the curriculum. Measuring happiness has its own problems, in that happiness is subjective and may fluctuate depending on what is happening in our lives and how we feel on that day. Researchers have found, however, that – even with these fluctuations – there is a link between emotional happiness and physical wellbeing. In terms of the country as a whole, in 2015 the UK was ranked twenty-third out of 157 countries.[28] Key factors for happiness include life expectancy, social-support networks and freedom to make choices.

The authors of the *World Happiness Report* argue that one of the keys to happiness is having a strong moral and ethical framework. This used to come from religious belief, but although 59 per cent of the world population describe themselves as religious, the proportion has

---

28 Helliwell, J., Layard, R. and Sachs, J. (eds) (2016) *World Happiness Report: 2016 Update.* New York: Sustainable Development Solutions Network.

fallen in most parts of the world and that trend is likely to continue. 'Where religious belief declines, a new view of ethics emerges. The rules of behaviour are then seen as made by man rather than by God in order to improve the quality of our human life together,' the report observes.

In other words, we are perhaps struggling to find the ethical framework that works for us in this fast-moving, challenging world. This is clear from looking at social media and online interaction, where people who would think twice before saying something unkind to someone in real life feel free to troll and harass others from behind the safety of a computer. The only deterrent is banning, it seems, rather than educating or giving guidelines. The *World Happiness Report* continues: 'Clearly there has developed to a degree, a moral vacuum into which have stepped some quite unwholesome ideas.' The report suggests that these unwholesome ideas include competition, personal success and a 'me' culture in which we expect to succeed simply because we want to and we don't mind whom we injure or ignore in the process.

This has real implications for how and what we teach in PSHE. Morals, values and ethics will be very much influenced by family, culture and society, but as teachers we also have a role to play in supporting children in developing critical thinking skills. It can seem that today's meritocratic culture is very much measured in exam passes, possessions, wealth and health, and while these can certainly be important keys to happiness, they must be balanced with positive relationships, empathy and doing good.

The *World Happiness Report* again reminds us that 'it is the human instinct to co-operate that has given humans their extraordinary power over most other vertebrate species'. In other words, one of the keys to happiness is our positive relationships with others. Of course, we have two sides to our natures – the selfish and the altruistic – and happiness involves self-compassion as well as compassion towards others. In a planned programme of PSHE that includes learning about happiness, it's important not only to develop the feeling of self-worth but also to explore the feelings of wellbeing associated with helping other people and developing positive relationships.

It has long been recognised that 'Happiness fuels success, not the other way round'.[29] Confident young people who have the skills to manage their relationships, to take risks and to think creatively may be in a better position to pursue success – in the words of the old adage, money can't necessarily buy happiness.

Happiness is a key human emotion and should be explored as part of the PSHE curriculum. Whether you draw that out into a planned programme as Wellington College has done depends on the needs of your pupils and how you structure PSHE in your school. Considering happiness may be part of teaching and learning about broader feelings, being able to describe, recognise and empathise. Developing skills around managing our feelings and empathising with the feelings of others should be at the heart of a PSHE curriculum so that we help children develop skills in managing their own feelings, guide them in developing their own ethical and moral boundaries, and help them challenge those 'unwholesome ideas'.

❋ SOMETHING TO THINK ABOUT

Is developing or adopting a programme of happiness as part of your planned programme of PSHE right for you? Action for Happiness has developed a schools programme which has been awarded the PSHE Association's Quality Mark. It is based around their member pledge to 'try and create more happiness and less unhappiness in the world around us', and this would be a good place to start.

Alternatively, note where the concept and practical application of happiness can be drawn out of your current programme of PSHE. Consider whether you fully address aspects of personal happiness and altruism, both within PSHE and across the school.

Do you ever measure happiness in school? Whole-school surveys such as those offered by the Schools and Health Education Unit will help you establish an insight into the pupils in your school and establish a baseline for further planning.

---

29 Lyubomirsky, S., King, L. and Diener, E. (2005) 'The benefits of frequent positive affect: Does happiness lead to success?' *Psychological Bulletin 131*, 6, 803–855.

● CASE STUDY ─────────────────────────────

Following on from training from Action for Happiness we were taught the idea of finishing the day by asking the children to reflect on three good things that had happened to them or simply three good things they could think of. This is something I do every day, and at my children's school they have been provided with diaries in which they record their 'three good things'. As a parent of a very anxious ten-year-old I've already noticed huge improvements in his attitude to school.

Teacher and parent

Answering tricky questions

Many teachers are anxious about teaching some of these trickier aspects of PSHE as they're worried about answering awkward questions and dealing with tricky topics. This is perfectly understandable when teaching topics like RSE, mental health and drugs and alcohol, so as always it's best to be prepared. Perhaps the topics may not be within your scope of knowledge and understanding, so you may cross your fingers and dread the moment someone's hand waggles in the air, just in case they're about to ask an awkward question. Before you were a teacher, though, perhaps you weren't 100 per cent sure what a fronted adverbial clause was, maybe you couldn't always remember the exact difference between integers and denominators, and possibly you would have been hard pushed to describe the differences between a Monet and a Manet. As a professional, however, you now know that knowledge is power, and you wouldn't start a lesson on Egyptian gods unless you had a fair idea about who and what they were.

The same goes for PSHE topics. Before attempting a potentially sensitive subject area – let's say, the changes that happen during puberty – you need to be totally familiar with the resources, the lesson objectives and the outcomes. You'll have set the ground rules with the class and these will be displayed clearly. At the beginning of the lesson you'll have reminded pupils what these ground rules are and recapped on learning so far. You'll have completed a baseline activity to establish where children are with their learning, and you've introduced the topic and started to deliver the teaching part.

A hand waggles in the air.

A pupil asks a question you weren't expecting and the class waits in hushed silence. It's not something you were planning to cover in this lesson, so what now?

- Listen to the question and acknowledge that you've heard it.

  - 'Thank you for asking that.'

  - 'That's an interesting question.'

- Explain when you'll be answering their question.

  - 'That's helpful for the whole class to know, so let's stop for a moment and talk about it.'

  - 'We need to get on with this activity right now, but let's come back to it at the end of the lesson.'

  - 'It's not something we're going to be covering in this lesson, but let's chat about that afterwards.'

  - 'We're not doing that in this lesson, but we'll be covering that next week.'

This can buy you some time for thinking, but always acknowledge the question and tell the child when you will deal with it. If any questions are personal, refer the child to the ground rules about asking about personal information, but always treat the questions with respect and seriousness, even if a pupil seems to be asking something silly. It may be something important or worrying to them. Then:

- If the question is about something that you won't be teaching in this lesson but that you'll be covering later, explain when you'll be covering it and how the question will be answered then.

- If the question is about something you're not covering in this set or module of lessons but that will be covered next year, then explain that this is not something you'll be working on now but their question will be answered next term or next year.

- If the question is not relevant to the topic, then have a chat with the child after the lesson to find out more about why they were asking that question now.

Once the lesson is over, ask to have a friendly chat with the child and ask them to repeat their question in a relaxed, non-confrontational way. Always ensure that you're following your school's child protection or safeguarding guidelines.

- Clarify what they want to know.
  - 'Can you explain a bit more about your question?'
  - 'What made you ask that question?'
  - 'Where did you hear that?'
- Decide whether the question is relevant and age-appropriate or a matter of safeguarding.
- Acknowledge their question again and say what you will do now. You could:
  - answer the question simply and factually
  - refer them to another colleague
  - refer them to their parents (and then make sure you chat with the parents, so that they understand what you have already said)
  - say that you need to chat to another member of staff about their question.

Don't sit tight and hope that the question will go away or that the questioner will forget about it. Deal with it either straight away in class or after class. It may be something that is troubling the child or it may be a red flag in terms of safeguarding. Equally, it may raise a concern that they're watching, listening to or taking part in age-inappropriate media (e.g. gaming or social media), and that needs to be tackled. Or maybe they thought it would embarrass you and make their friends laugh. If so, a chat is an opportunity to remind them of the ground rules and that 'respecting others' includes respecting you as the teacher and respecting others in the class.

Have some simple script answers already planned, such as those in the suggestions above. Find what works for you, act respectfully and assertively towards the child, and always keep confidentiality and safeguarding guidelines in mind.

Inviting questions with a question box or 'ask-it basket'

It's worth having a forum where children can ask questions privately, too. This may be in the form of a question box or an 'ask-it basket' – a box, tin or basket where children can post their questions. At the end of a PSHE lesson, give pupils time to write down any questions they may have and invite them to pop their questions in the box.

In order to make things fair, offer a slip of paper or Post-it® note to each child and give them time to write a question. If they have no question, they can simply write 'No question'. Some teachers like to address questions there and then in the classroom, but it's probably easier to read the questions after the lesson and prepare your answers for the next session. Sometimes children don't have a question but just want to share a little story or an idea with you. Question boxes are a good way of ensuring that all pupils are able to ask their questions in a safe way and allow you as the teacher to check understanding and to clarify any misunderstanding.

Some teachers offer anonymity for pupils posting questions, but what if a child discloses something in their question and you're not able to identify and support them? You'll probably recognise the writing anyway, but just in case it may be better to ask pupils to put their initials on their slip of paper. Reassure them that their questions will remain confidential in terms of sharing them with the class, but that you may need to speak to someone about their question if you have a concern. Remind pupils that their questions will never be the subject of general chat or gossip. If pupils are younger or need some extra support, then offer to scribe the question for them or ask another member of staff to help with scribing.

● CASE STUDY ─────────────────────────

Following a series of lessons on puberty with my Year Five class, I asked pupils to write down their questions and put them in the class question box. There was a question in the box from a girl asking if she should shave her legs because she was being teased about having hairy legs. I'd allowed the children to post their questions anonymously but luckily I recognised the girl's handwriting. We were able to have a chat about her worries and she agreed that I could also chat to her parents about this. Together we reassured the child that she was under no pressure to do anything and she promised to talk to her mum about any fears in the future. We were able to have a class discussion on general name calling and body image issues without referring to the original issue. This was something that had really worried and upset this child, and she was so relieved she had been able to ask advice in a safe way.

Year Five teacher

❋ SOMETHING TO THINK ABOUT

Devise your own script for managing tricky questions and practise it. Make a question box or 'ask-it basket' for your classroom and explain to pupils how it works. Leave it in class all the time and check it at regular intervals or bring it out for PSHE lessons. For further reading, have a look at the PSHE Association's *Handling Sensitive or Controversial Issues*[30] or the NSPCC's *Talking About Difficult Topics* (www.nspcc.org.uk/preventing-abuse/keeping-children-safe/talking-about-difficult-topics).

Linking PSHE and Science

We've already seen how PSHE can be closely linked to other subject areas to create consistent messages across school, but Science has naturally close links and needs more careful exploration. While Science is based in knowledge, discovery and developing enquiry, PSHE has a slightly different spin in that it's about pulling out some of the elements and exploring the 'why' behind them.

Mapping the occasions where Science and PSHE link, overlap and support each other will help make learning more consistent and cohesive and will eliminate unnecessary repetition. Table 3.3 shows how one strand of the Science curriculum, 'Animals including humans', is closely interconnected with the PSHE Association's Core Theme One, 'Health and wellbeing'. The PSHE elements link very closely to Science but offer pupils the chance to explore the topics in a slightly different way.

---

30 PSHE Association (2012) *Handling Sensitive or Controversial Issues.* London: PSHE Association.

Table 3.3 Mapping links between the Science curriculum and PSHE

	Science: 'Animals including humans'	PSHE Association: Core Theme One: 'Health and wellbeing'
Year One	Pupils should be taught to: • identify, name, draw and label the basic parts of the human body and say which part of the body is associated with each sense. Notes and guidance (non-statutory): *Pupils should have plenty of opportunities to learn the names of the main body parts (including head, neck, arms, elbow, legs, knees, face, ears, eyes, hair, mouth, teeth) through games, actions, songs and rhymes.*	• what constitutes a healthy lifestyle including the benefits of physical activity, rest, healthy eating and dental health • to recognise what they like and dislike, how to make real, informed choices that improve their physical and emotional health, to recognise that choices can have good and not so good consequences • the importance of and how to maintain personal hygiene • how some diseases are spread and can be controlled and the responsibilities they have for their own health and that of others • about the process of growing from young to old and how people's needs change • about growing and changing and new opportunities and responsibilities that increasing independence may bring • the names for the main parts of the body (including external genitalia) • the similarities and differences between boys and girls
Year Two	Pupils should be taught to: • notice that animals, including humans, have offspring which grow into adults • find out about and describe the basic needs of animals, including humans, for survival (water, food and air) • describe the importance for humans of exercise, eating the right amounts of different types of food, and hygiene. Notes and guidance (non-statutory): *Pupils should be introduced to the basic needs of animals for survival, as well as the importance of exercise and nutrition for humans. They should also be introduced to the processes of reproduction and growth in animals. The focus at this stage should be on questions that help pupils to recognise growth; they should not be expected to understand how reproduction occurs.* *The following examples might be used: egg, chick, chicken; egg, caterpillar, pupa, butterfly; spawn, tadpole, frog; lamb, sheep. Growing into adults can include reference to baby, toddler, child, teenager, adult.* *Pupils might work scientifically by: observing, through video or first-hand observation and measurement, how different animals, including humans, grow; asking questions about what things animals need for survival and what humans need to stay healthy; and suggesting ways to find answers to their questions*	

Year Three	Pupils should be taught to: • identify that animals, including humans, need the right types and amount of nutrition, and that they cannot make their own food; they get nutrition from what they eat • identify that humans and some other animals have skeletons and muscles for support, protection and movement. Notes and guidance (non-statutory): *Pupils should continue to learn about the importance of nutrition and should be introduced to the main body parts associated with the skeleton and muscles, finding out how different parts of the body have special functions.* *Pupils might work scientifically by: identifying and grouping animals with and without skeletons and observing and comparing their movement; exploring ideas about what would happen if humans did not have skeletons. They might compare and contrast the diets of different animals (including their pets) and decide ways of grouping them according to what they eat. They might research different food groups and how they keep us healthy, and design meals based on what they find out.*	• what positively and negatively affects their physical, mental and emotional health (including the media) • how to make informed choices (including recognising that choices can have positive, neutral and negative consequences) and to begin to understand the concept of a 'balanced lifestyle' • to recognise opportunities to make their own choices about food, what might influence their choices and the benefits of eating a balanced diet
Year Four	Pupils should be taught to: • describe the simple functions of the basic parts of the digestive system in humans • identify the different types of teeth in humans and their simple functions • construct and interpret a variety of food chains, identifying producers, predators and prey. Notes and guidance (non-statutory): *Pupils should be introduced to the main body parts associated with the digestive system, for example, mouth, tongue, teeth, oesophagus, stomach, and small and large intestine, and explore questions that help them to understand their special functions.* *Pupils might work scientifically by: comparing the teeth of carnivores and herbivores and suggesting reasons for differences; finding out what damages teeth and how to look after them. They might draw and discuss their ideas about the digestive system and compare them with models or images.*	• about change, including transitions (between Key Stages and schools), loss, separation, divorce and bereavement • that bacteria and viruses can affect health and that following simple routines can reduce their spread
Year Five	Pupils should be taught to: • describe the changes as humans develop to old age. Notes and guidance (non-statutory): *Pupils should draw a timeline to indicate stages in the growth and development of humans. They should learn about the changes experienced in puberty.* *Pupils could work scientifically by researching the gestation periods of other animals and comparing them with humans; by finding out and recording the length and mass of a baby as it grows.*	• which, why and how commonly available substances and drugs (including alcohol and tobacco) could damage their immediate and future health and safety, that some are legal, some are restricted and some are illegal to own, use and supply to others

cont.

		• how their body will change as they approach and move through puberty • about human reproduction • about people who are responsible for helping them stay healthy and safe and ways that they can help these people
Year Six	Pupils should be taught to: • identify and name the main parts of the human circulatory system, and describe the functions of the heart, blood vessels and blood • recognise the impact of diet, exercise, drugs and lifestyle on the way their bodies function • describe the ways in which nutrients and water are transported within animals, including humans. Notes and guidance (non-statutory): *Pupils should build on their learning from years 3 and 4 about the main body parts and internal organs (skeletal, muscular and digestive system) to explore and answer questions that help them to understand how the circulatory system enables the body to function.* *Pupils should learn how to keep their bodies healthy and how their bodies might be damaged – including how some drugs and other substances can be harmful to the human body.* *Pupils might work scientifically by: exploring the work of scientists and scientific research about the relationship between diet, exercise, drugs, lifestyle and health.*	

Department for Education (2013) Science Programmes of Study: Key Stages 1 and 2, National Curriculum in England. London: Department for Education; PSHE Association (2017) Programme of Study. London: PSHE Association

Pupils often complain that 'We did that in Science' when it comes to topics like healthy eating and puberty, so it's important to map how and where topics are being taught. Let's take growing and changing as an example. The Year Five Science notes and guidance (non-statutory) states that pupils

should learn about the changes experienced in puberty.

In terms of Science this may mean learning about the physical changes that boys and girls go through in puberty. Children may learn about hormones, growth and change and the development of adult characteristics.

The PSHE Association's *Programme of Study* suggests that pupils should learn

> *how their body will change as they approach and move through puberty.*

This is almost identical to the Science element but, in addition, pupils should have the opportunity to learn:

- what positively and negatively affects their physical, mental and emotional health (including the media)

- about people who are responsible for helping them stay healthy and safe and ways that they can help these people.

There are also more programme elements in Core Theme Two, 'Relationships'.

Building on the Science requirements, you can create a set of lessons and learning experiences that put the scientific changes into context, offer pupils the chance to explore some ideas around responsibility and changing relationships, and check where to seek help if they need it. Carefully planning PSHE and Science together can help ensure that both subjects support and enhance each other, leading to a more comprehensive coverage of your topic. It also means that you don't waste precious PSHE curriculum time in delivering aspects that are better suited to the Science curriculum.

As a Key Stage 1 example, let's consider the following statement from the *Science Programmes of Study*. Pupils should be taught to

> *describe the importance for humans of exercise, eating the right amounts of different types of food, and hygiene.*

This matches with the PSHE elements from Core Theme One that pupils should learn:

- what constitutes a healthy lifestyle including the benefits of physical activity, rest, healthy eating and dental health

- to recognise what they like and dislike, how to make real, informed choices that improve their physical and emotional health, to recognise that choices can have good and not so good consequences

- the importance of and how to maintain personal hygiene.

There's a real synergy between the two curricula: pupils learn about healthy foods and exercise (knowledge), and then explore their likes and dislikes and make choices (skills, attitudes and understanding) and how to maintain simple personal hygiene (skills).

Taking a more joined-up approach to PSHE and Science means that it's possible to cover linked topics adequately from all angles (knowledge, skills and understanding). This can help in making sure PSHE is not seen as a bolt-on and can help raise its profile as an essential part of the school curriculum.

Responding to national and international incidents

While PSHE should be carefully planned, as we've already seen, there is also a need to add in a degree of flexibility so that you can respond to national and international events. If an attack or major incident occurs and whether your school is in or near the incident or far away, children may be aware of the news coverage or hear adults talking about their concerns.

Should teachers spend some time talking about such incidents and, if so, *how* do we talk to children about them? The key as always is to tailor your discussion to the age and needs of your pupils. You know your pupils best and you are an adult figure they can trust. As with all PSHE teaching and learning (even if it's just a discussion rather than a lesson), set some simple ground rules to give the discussion parameters and to set the scene.

It's important that children feel able to express their fears and anxieties, so ensure that they can talk about their concerns. Using the ground rules checklist, make sure that the discussion sticks to simple facts and don't allow the discussion to go down the route of 'My dad says that…' or 'My mum thinks that…' so that you can avoid speculation, rumour and gossip. If you're not sure what the facts are, check the local police force statements or news from a reliable source.

Reassure children that, although it may seem that there are lots of scary incidents going on, attacks are fairly rare and it is unlikely that something like this will happen to them or their families. It's good to talk about their fears and concerns, but remind them that talking about rumours and gossip or frightening and teasing others may upset them and make them more scared.

If there has been an act of extremism, some groups of children may feel that they are under scrutiny because of their faith or culture, and it's important to support and reassure these children and their families too. You may want to mark the event by having a class or school acknowledgement such as a silence or a special assembly.

If children ask why, answer them simply and honestly. Childhood bereavement charity Winston's Wish suggests the following wording,[31] but you will have your own way of answering:

> No-one can completely know why. We know it wasn't an accident. It's so, so difficult to understand why anyone would be so cruel as to kill (or hurt) other people.

Remind children that there are adults they can talk to if they feel scared, worried or sad and help them identify these adults in school and at home. If it seems appropriate, offer to be in the classroom at break time if anyone wants to stay and chat, or suggest that each child think of one trusted adult in school they could talk to and one trusted adult out of school. It's okay to acknowledge your own feelings of sadness, too. Make sure you are also able to chat about your own concerns or fears to a colleague, friend or family member. Your own mental health and wellbeing is equally important.

The same advice goes for any natural disasters. Reassure children and answer their questions simply and factually. Some children may want to fundraise for charity in response to a natural disaster so that they can feel that they are doing something proactive. While it's not possible to fundraise or hold charity events for every problem, if children want to do their bit then this may help them make sense of their concerns. Perhaps they can organise and hold an event and also have a hand in running it. If there really isn't time, then an article in the school newsletter could have an offer to act as a point of contact for any families who want to contribute to charity fundraising, or point to a local organisation that can help. While we don't want children to worry unduly about world events, it's important to acknowledge their concerns, as these are a part of their developing empathy and becoming an active citizen in the community.

Not all world events are disasters, of course. Elections and major changes offer an opportunity to explore the democratic process and how to deal with feelings if your chosen party or representative doesn't get elected. Again, talk about events using factual language

---

31 Winston's Wish: *Responding to Children Affected by the Media Coverage of the Incident at Westminster.* Accessed on 4 January 2018 from www.winstonswish.org.uk/responding-children-affected-media-coverage-incident-westminster.

and avoid speculating. At election time, hold class or school elections: encourage pupils to stand for election and to develop policies and manifestos, and then hold hustings. This will help pupils develop their understanding of democracy. Even the youngest children can begin to understand the democratic process.

● CASE STUDY

It was election time and I wanted my Reception class to learn more about the process. I divided the class into small groups and they had to agree on a party name and what they stood for. When they had chosen, they created manifesto posters (the Chocolate Party – chocolate for all!; the Climbing Trees Party – children should be allowed to climb trees more!) using drawing and writing and shared these with the rest of the class. Each member of the 'party' spoke and shared their pride in their shared ideas. We made rosettes and held hustings, and when it came time to vote, each child had to put their cross on their voting slip and put it in the sealed box. Returning Officers counted the votes and announced the winners. The children understood that this was a fun learning activity but had a real interest in the election process. Several accompanied their parents to the polls and all wanted to discuss the results and who had been elected. Through this one activity we covered elements of English and Maths and understanding the world.

Reception teacher

✷ SOMETHING TO THINK ABOUT

For more information, read the PSHE Association's *Discussing a Terrorist Attack with Children in Primary Phase.*[32]

---

32 PSHE Association (2017) *Discussing a Terrorist Attack with Children in Primary Phase.* London: PSHE Association.

• Chapter Four •

MAKING PSHE OUTSTANDING

Now we've looked at the building blocks of PSHE, this chapter will help you begin to scaffold outstanding PSHE lessons within the parameters of the PSHE Association's 'Ten Principles of PSHE Education' (see the Appendix). Starting from the ground up, we'll start to structure and build PSHE lessons that aren't just okay or good but outstanding.

Building outstanding lessons

Think about the best lesson you ever taught – the one where everything went like clockwork, the children responded and there was clear learning going on. What happened for that lesson to go so well? What did you do in that lesson? How did the children respond?

In order for PSHE lessons to be aspirational, challenging and ultimately outstanding, they will need to be planned and delivered in the same way as that dream lesson. First you'll recap and review on what the children have aleady covered in this topic – or, if it's a new topic, you might run a simple baseline activity. You'll need to know your subject content and to have an engaging way of delivering the instructional section using a talk, a presentation, a scenario, a film clip, a story or some other stimulus. There may be a discussion element in which you can expand on the topic, clarify any misunderstandings and address any gaps. You'll check for understanding at various points, and then go on to an activity where the children can develop and practise their skills. Next you'll recap together and review pupils' learning, perhaps with an opportunity for assessment. You may give pupils a takeaway task – something they need to do or a skill they need to practise – and finally you'll tell them about the next steps in what you'll be learning together.

First things first. Before moving on to the main lesson part, let's set some ground rules.

Setting ground rules

While setting ground rules at the beginning of a topic or module of PSHE learning might sometimes seem like a faff, it's an essential part of the process. Ground rules allow pupils and staff to set parameters and gives all involved a sense of belonging and of safety. Setting ground rules is a process that brings a group or a class together, ready to learn.

You may already have class rules that you set together at the beginning of the school year, but PSHE ground rules are a little more specialised. The aim is to create the conditions that will allow discussion of the sensitive topics that arise in PSHE and that will allow children to feel safe while learning, and you to feel safe while teaching. While ground rules can and should reflect the needs of your class and the topic being covered, there are some givens that need to be covered as a matter of safeguarding.

Confidentiality

It's important that those who participate in the session understand their role in terms of confidentiality. That is: children must understand that away from the classroom they should not frighten others or gossip about topics they've been learning about in class or anything their peers have said. The learning but not the content of the lessons should be discussed.

Confidentiality, however, comes with safeguarding caveats. Pupils need to understand that if they disclose anything that might constitute an issue of safeguarding or child protection, then the teacher has a duty of care to report that to the school's DSL. Reassure the children that this will never be an issue for general discussion among staff but that you will deal with the matter carefully in accordance with the school's safeguarding policy.

Teachers often worry about confidentiality issues in relation to particularly sensitive lessons such as those about consent or drugs and alcohol. Having clear guidelines in place means that if the questions or the discussion veer into difficult territory, the teacher leading the session can always refer back to the ground rules. Always refer to your school's child protection or safeguarding policy.

Respect

We use the word 'respect' a lot in schools. We must respect the rules, each other and property. We often assume that children know and understand about respect, but it's an abstract concept: perhaps we could explain it to them so that they have a fuller understanding of what it means. For example, ground rules might contain instructions to 'respect others' feelings and opinions'. Give examples, explore the concept of respect, and try to find a class definition. 'Respect' can be defined as 'Due regard for the feelings, wishes, or rights of others' (*Oxford English Dictionary*) – what will this look like and feel like in your class?

No personal questions

This needs to be made explicit so that personal stories are kept out of the session and there is no discussion about a named person. Pupils may want to know whether a teacher has experienced something you're discussing or about the teacher's personal view on a situation. It's important that discussions are neutral, and in this context distancing (which we'll look at later in this chapter) is a useful technique. If a pupil asks a personal question of the teacher or another pupil, they can simply be reminded of the rules.

It's okay to pass

Not everyone will want to discuss the topics being covered and some will feel shy or unsure about sharing their ideas. That's okay – everyone has a right to pass. In planning the lesson, however, ensure that it includes active learning techniques, so that everyone has a chance to take part in whichever form works best for them. Encourage active participation as much as possible, but you'll be able to recognise the difference between a pupil who can't be bothered to think or take part and one who may be anxious about saying something.

Vocabulary

Words should be used carefully and respectfully. Pupils also need to be aware of using the correct terminology when talking about topics such as RSE. Check that you yourself are using up-to-date language for drugs and alcohol, such as 'psychoactive substances' rather than 'legal highs'. Check the Mentor-ADEPIS website for the latest information.

Asking for help

Always indicate where pupils can go after the session to get further information and advice. You might offer your own availability – 'I'll be in the classroom at 1.30 if anyone needs to come and talk to me' – or you might signpost school-based or local services, or national support such as Childline. As part of the session you may talk about people in our families and in the school community who can help us.

Creating the ground rules

So how do we actually *create* these ground rules? The most straightforward way to create a set of ground rules is to ask the pupils themselves to suggest some rules, or adding rules you'd like that the children haven't thought of (perhaps prompting them to think of them). Ask pairs to think of one key rule they'd like to contribute and to say it or to write it on a Post-it® note. You can eliminate doubles and help sort the rules into order of importance. The problem with this method is that children will often call out the things they think you want to hear and it can turn into a long list of *don'ts* – don't shout out, don't laugh, don't disturb others, don't mess about, don't be rude, don't walk around, and so on. Encourage pupils to put a positive spin on the suggestions so that you get a list of what we *should* be doing – listen carefully when someone is talking, respect others' opinions, try your best, and so on.

When using these suggestions, be careful of any disconnect between words and actions. It's easy to say what we should be doing, but it's not always easy to stick to the rules in practice. It's the difference between knowing what we should do and actually doing it. Give examples of what each rule might look like in action or ask pupils to come up with their own examples. What might encourage pupils to stick to their suggestions?

Once you have a list of rules, try to combine them and cut them down to no more than five or six. For example, 'Listen to the teacher' and 'Listen to each other' could be grouped as 'Listen to the person who is talking'.

Another method is to ask for the opposite of a set of ground rules. On a flipchart or whiteboard so that everyone can see what you're writing, ask the children to imagine the worst-ever PSHE lesson. What are the pupils doing? What is happening or not happening? What does it feel like to be in this awful classroom? Be imaginative and creative. Pupils might gleefully suggest that people are shouting, the equipment is being thrown around and everyone is laughing at each other. Allow the children to go to town with their suggestions. One that seems to come up on a regular basis is someone setting fire to the bin! Once you have your list of misdemeanours, start to reverse them. Cross out the negative suggestion and ask pupils to reverse it into a positive suggestion. Write this in a different-coloured pen above the bad behaviour. Thus, 'Throwing equipment around the room' becomes 'We look after the equipment', and 'Laughing at each other' becomes 'We respect each other's opinions'. And the fire in the bin? What about 'We make sure that PSHE lessons are safe for all'?

This method tends to work well with pupils: they create a picture of what happens in a chaotic classroom and then reverse it so as to visualise a well-functioning PSHE lesson. Again, though, make sure that there are only five or six rules by the end, and check that they incorporate the suggestions above about confidentiality and signposting to additional support after the session.

For another way of creating a positive learning environment or developing ground rules, let's go back to that issue of respect. Write the word 'Respect' in the middle of the board and ask pupils to discuss what it means. Ask for examples of respect in action in the classroom and the playground. Ask pupils to discuss in pairs or small groups what 'respect' might mean or look like in a PSHE session, and jot down their ideas on the board. They will probably come up with a similar list of ground rules, such as 'Respect others' opinions', 'Respect the person talking' or 'Respect the equipment and resources'. Check that you have the key issues covered; this can form the basis of your set of ground rules. When reminding pupils of any of the rules, you then only need to use that one word, 'Respect' – because they've gone through the process of unpicking what that means, they'll have a better concept of what it looks like in the context of PSHE.

Whatever process you use, you will have created a (short) set of ground rules that have meaning for you and your class. These should be displayed at the beginning of every session with a quick recap and a check of understanding. If any need to be added over time then do add them, but be careful about creating a list of prohibitive decrees. The aim of ground rules is to set the parameters for safety and comfort for all involved and to create the conditions for safe, effective learning.

Safeguarding and confidentiality in PSHE

Safeguarding and child protection are non-negotiable, of course, and they may be the reason why some teachers feel anxious about PSHE. While there might be disclosures and tricky topics in Geography or Maths, for example, if you're talking about topics such as bullying, alcohol or sex then clearly there is much greater scope for potentially tricky conversations.

This is why it's so important to lay the foundations first. Safeguarding and confidentiality should always be part of the ground rules in words and language that the children understand. If you skip the ground-rules stage, you won't have that framework and boundary in place. Creating a safe, open atmosphere in your classroom so that you can support children in their understanding and skills development is an important part too, as is ensuring that pupils are able to ask questions, either during the lesson or afterwards. The chain of support following a lesson is crucial.

One key point in the ground rules relating to confidentiality is the right to pass. If a child doesn't wish to answer a question or to take part in a particular discussion, then it's okay for them to listen and engage in other ways. They should not be pressurised into joining in in ways that feel uncomfortable to them (although it's still important that they engage in other ways).

Never make assumptions about what a child is saying or what you think they *might* be saying. Ask questions to clarify what they've said, during the lesson if appropriate or in a one-to-one chat afterwards. Stay as neutral as possible.

Remind pupils that what they are learning in this lesson is for children of their age and their stage of learning. It's important, therefore, that the lesson stays in the room and that pupils don't gossip in the playground or try to frighten or tease younger children. Remind them that as the teacher you will also respect this, and that what is said in class won't become staffroom chat. The only exception to this is if you feel concerned about something and need to talk to another member of staff, but this will be done in private and you will let the child know whom you have talked to.

Remind children that they can ask questions and where in school they can go for help after the lesson. If they have something worrying or troubling them, then this may be a better setting for them to talk about it than in the lesson itself.

All adults involved in teaching or supporting PSHE – teaching support staff, governors, visitors, members of external agencies working with the school, and parents – need to understand their role in safeguarding and confidentiality and the steps they can take if they have any concerns.

Check that all PSHE-related policies have clear steps and guidelines on disclosure that follow the latest safeguarding and child-protection guidance and that match the school's own safeguarding policy. If you don't already have a separate confidentiality policy, consider creating one. Include key information about where to find PSHE teaching and learning guidance (including techniques such as distancing), reference to school and national guidance, and steps to take if a child discloses to you. Add in key information about ground rules and the importance of well-planned ground rules for PSHE lessons. Make sure that the confidentiality policy is available to parents and carers and is discussed and reviewed by governors.

Creating distance

While we're still considering the preparation stage, it's important to recap on distancing. PSHE needs to be a safe space in which to develop, practise and consolidate new skills. It's an opportunity for pupils to experience these skills before encountering them in real life, and distancing helps to make these experiences less personal. Ground rules are the starting point, but the idea of distancing is to remove the personal from situations that may be sensitive for pupils. Instead of asking children to examine their own personal experiences, you can create distance by using characters and stories instead. This will help pupils to express themselves freely and safely. They can explore their own and others' points of views in an open and safe way, and then relate the ideas to their own lives and experiences.

One of the easiest ways of using distancing is to use scenarios and stories. As the teacher you can create scenarios and characters that are appropriate to the children's age and experience but that are one step removed. Rather than asking pupils to recall a time when they were bullied or witnessed bullying in the playground, you can set the scene by putting another character in that situation. Picture books and novels can also provide good starting points – almost all books for children contain some kind of PSHE-related learning or dilemma. You can link learning to the texts the children are studying in English. Use empathy, problem-solving, hot-seating and freeze-frame (discussed below) to help pupils understand characters' motivations and to offer advice on dilemmas. Extend the learning by placing a well-known character in a different situation and giving them advice.

For younger pupils, puppets can help you present a problem to be solved. Create a scenario or story around a favourite puppet or toy and ask the children to help that character. Again, this can be explored through drama, through discussion or through individual, paired or group work. Once pupils have an understanding of a new topic you can consolidate learning and check for understanding by using a problem-solving technique. Giving pupils a story in which a character has a problem means that they have to grasp the problem, consider their response based on what they know and understand, and then offer a solution. The solutions can be presented as verbal feedback, as a short drama or in written form. You can assess pupils' understanding and address any problems.

Introducing a topic

Think about the best way to introduce your particular topic. This may be as simple as talking about it, or showing a picture, a film clip, a book or some other stimulus. You may want to present a new topic as a question or statement to get pupils thinking: 'What makes a good friend?', 'Why is Teddy sad today?', 'Eating healthily is a waste of time.' 'What is the difference between bullying and arguing?' You might start the lesson with a challenge or a quest: 'If you had to make a recipe for friendship, what would you put in?', 'How would you describe human emotions to an alien?', 'What advice would a leaflet on growing up need to contain?', 'Teddy wants to get healthy. Can you help?', 'Make a first-aid kit for someone who is worried.'

These questions can also arise from watching a short film clip, reading a poem, a picture book or an extract from a novel, or showing a presentation, all of which may lead into a further activity or discussion.

Using discussion techniques

Discussion is a really useful tool in PSHE and can be used to gauge understanding and views, to establish baselines and to encourage debate around a topic. All too often, however, discussion ends up being aimless and unfocused. Discussion is usually led by the teacher, who guides and directs it and who ultimately chooses which children engage and which children are heard.

This is one method, but there are other ways of engaging *all* pupils in discussion and creating a meaningful learning opportunity. These methods can be used in every subject – they are not restricted to PSHE. The best thing about these different models of discussion is that they remove the teacher from the role of lead adult and instead allow children to participate fully – which also then leaves you free to observe and support. The methods can be adjusted, depending on the age of your pupils. Younger pupils may need more adult guidance, but with prompting and practice even the youngest can begin to lead their own discussion. Discussion is not meant to replace the teaching section of a lesson but may be used to start pupils thinking at the beginning of a topic, to help them delve deeper into what they're learning and to help consolidate learning.

When planning a lesson that has an element of discussion, be clear about what you want to achieve and what exactly the outcome will be for the children:

- Every child will have the opportunity to contribute to creating a class charter on friendship, using think–pair–share.

Or:

- Each group of four pupils will come up with three ingredients that are key to friendship.

Rather than:

- Hold a discussion on what makes a good friendship.

The following ideas are just some suggestions, with examples. Older children can take part independently, especially as they get used to the different methods. Younger children may need adult support to get going, but it's important to encourage pupils to talk about ideas in their group so that they don't just speak via the adult. As the teacher leading the lessons, you can use the methods that work for you or the ones that work best with your pupils, or you can create your own ideas.

What all these ideas offer is the chance to have a focused discussion so that talk is purposeful and meaningful. Remind pupils of the ground rules (including the rule about not sharing personal stories) and encourage all to participate and to actively listen when others are speaking.

Chat stations

Divide the class into groups and set up a question and a stimulus photograph or picture at different 'stations' (areas, tables, etc.) around the room. The photograph or picture might be the same at each station but with a different question for each. Give groups a set amount of time (use a stopwatch or a timer app) to discuss the question, and then ask each group to move to the next station. You could also ask them to add notes or jot down their ideas on paper as an aide-mémoire.

Each group will have had some time at each station, so when you come together as a class and talk about the topic they will all have had similar experiences but the small group size will have encouraged engagement and participation. Spending a set amount of time (it need only be a few minutes) on each topic will also encourage children to think more deeply, beyond their initial thoughts.

● EXAMPLE

At the centre of each station is a photograph of the same person. Each photograph is accompanied by a different question, such as 'What is this person thinking?', 'What has just happened?', 'What is this person saying?' or 'What will happen next?'

Once everyone has visited all of the chat stations, you can gather up the photographs and talk about the range of answers.

Can pupils now create a 'feelings story' for that person? You could ask: 'Did your thoughts about this person change as you went along? What if you had gone with your original thoughts?'

Affinity-mapping

In groups, pupils are given a question or topic, and after a group discussion they must come up with some thoughts or ideas. You may want to suggest a set number and then ask them to write each idea, thought or question on a Post-it® note. Devise some overarching headlines and write these on flipchart paper (or on a board) and ask the groups to post their Post-it® notes under the heading that best fits.

● EXAMPLE

Ask groups to discuss what keeps us healthy, and to write down their top five things. Then ask them to post their notes under headings like 'Food and drink', 'Exercise' and 'Mental health'.

You can follow up by talking about any repetitions, gaps or questions.

(You might wish to photograph the diagrams for reference or future learning.)

Concentric circles or speed-dating

Divide the class into two sets and ask them to stand either in two concentric circles with the inner circle facing the outer one or just in two lines facing each other. If the class is too big, divide them into two or four sets and give them a separate space in the room.

One set of pupils has a question to ask and the other set will try to answer it, to give advice or just to discuss the question (depending on the topic). After a fixed amount of time (a minute or 90 seconds works well here), ask the circle or line to move on one step and ask their question to the next person. By the end of the set they'll have discussed their question or topic several times in several ways and they will have given and heard different viewpoints.

You can then come together and take feedback or decide as a class which advice seemed helpful.

● EXAMPLE ─────────────────────

Child One tells Child Two something they think is a risk. Child Two offers some advice on how to make the risk a safe one, and they discuss the answer. After a set amount of time, Child One moves on and asks Child Three the same question.

After a few turns, Child One has to decide which advice seemed best to them, and they can then check with the rest of the class or group.

Snowball discussions

In pairs, children talk about a topic or question; then, after a set amount of time, they link up with another pair and share their thoughts. The four children then link up with another group of four children and talk again. The idea is to start the discussion on a small scale and thus to encourage all pupils to participate and to have a chance to talk and be heard. They will need to be able to remember their discussion and explain it to the next larger group each time, and this helps to reinforce the information. At some point you're likely to end up with different numbers in groups, depending on the number of children in your class, but the main aim is to grow the group but keep the discussion based on the topic in hand.

● EXAMPLE ─────────────────────

Pairs talk about rules and laws they know that keep them safe.

Pairs get together. In a four, they recap on the rules and laws they know, and add in any new ones.

By the end, the group of 8 or 16 (or the whole class) should have a large set of rules and laws. You can then affinity-map these or simply make a note of them for discussion later.

Envoys

Pupils are divided into groups, and each group talks about a different topic or question. After a set amount of time, they send an envoy representing their discussion to another group. The envoy tells the new group what they have talked about and asks the new group to add any new thoughts for feedback. This can be repeated or left as just one pass.

This method encourages participation, debate, and careful listening when the envoy speaks.

● EXAMPLE

Each group is given one stimulus statement about friendship, such as: 'If a friend lets you down, you should never trust them again', 'It's harder to make new friends as you get older' or 'Friends should be able to sort out their differences on their own.'

Envoys talk about what their group thought and the new group listens carefully. The envoy then invites further ideas and takes those back to the home/first group.

Think–pair–share

This is a simple way of growing a discussion. Individuals think about a question or topic on their own for a short time. They then turn to the person next to them and share their thoughts and ideas. Pairs can then share these with the whole class or with another group.

● EXAMPLE

Ask individuals to think of three things that make a good friendship.

Ask each child to turn to the person next to them and share their three things. Which were the same? Which were different? As a pair, did they agree?

These ideas can then be used in the whole class to create a list of what makes a good friendship, and this can lead to looking at the suggestions and an activity on how we develop the skills of positive friendship.

Rainbow chats

Small groups are each given a topic or question to discuss and the group is given a colour. After a set amount of time, children must get into a new group of mixed colours (a rainbow) and share the ideas they talked about in their original group. It helps if you give pupils a coloured sticker or card so that they can quickly see where they might make a new group and not spend too much time wandering around! It's fine if there are two reds and a couple of greens in one group – it's unlikely that you'll get a perfect rainbow in each group. The idea is simply to mix up the groups and get them to share ideas and listen to each other's thoughts.

● EXAMPLE

Red Group comes up with some situations where conflict might arise in the playground; Yellow Group comes up with some conflict situations in the classroom; Green Group comes up with some ways of solving conflict; and Blue Group lists some of the feelings associated with conflict.

In rainbow groups, the children share the ideas from their group and talk about the other groups' ideas.

As a class, try and match up possible solutions with each problem or carry out some role-play in which children practise solving a common conflict.

❂ SOMETHING TO THINK ABOUT

Try out a method of discussion that is new to you and your class. Start simply and make your expectations clear. Be prepared to help iron out wrinkles in understanding or to manage the group in the first instance and reflect on what went well and what you might need to change next time. There are lots of different ways of managing discussions in class, and methods popular in business can easily be adapted for primary-age children, so find what works for you.

Using drama techniques

Some teachers shy away from using drama as they feel it's not their 'thing', but you really don't have to be an award-winning actor to use drama as an effective tool to consolidate learning and practise skills in PSHE. It's not just role-play, either – there are a range of techniques and drama games that get pupils interacting, developing empathy and most importantly practising the skills they've learnt in the safe environment of the classroom. The activity you choose will depend on your class, their age and the learning outcomes, but they are all active and put the children at the heart of the learning. Once you have delivered the teaching part of the lesson, a drama activity can help develop and consolidate skills further.

Hot-seating

This where a pupil or the teacher takes on a role and answers questions as that character. This may be a real or historical figure, a fictional character from a story, or a character in an imaginary scenario.

Give the character some time to get into role. Remind them to speak in the first person; think about how the character might sit and speak (don't worry about accents!), and the sort of words they might use. Encourage the audience of pupils to work in pairs to come up with questions. As a warm-up it's fine to start with simple closed questions, such as 'What is your name?', 'What is your age?' and 'What is your occupation?' The questioning can then develop into more complex open-ended quizzing. The aim is to find out about a scenario from multiple points of view, and the technique works best when different characters from the same story have the opportunity to be quizzed. If you're in the hot seat yourself you can elicit the sort of questioning you'd like the children to use. Hot-seating can be used with the very youngest children to develop skills of empathy, and right up to Year Six with more complex issues for which there may be multiple viewpoints.

● EXAMPLE

In this example, the teacher uses a figure about whom the children are learning in History as the focus in developing and practising skills around being assertive in a difficult situation.

The teacher is in the hot seat, taking the role of Grace Darling. Children ask questions about how she felt risking her life to rescue others and if she had any doubts about whether she was doing the right thing.

Now hot-seat Grace's father and ask how he felt when his daughter insisted on rescuing the stranded passengers from the shipwreck.

As a follow-up, ask small groups or pairs to practise their assertiveness skills in imagined scenarios.

Hot-seating is best for:

- developing skills of empathy

- presenting multiple viewpoints for one situation

- initiating engagement from all pupils.

Freeze-frame and thought-tracking

With this technique, you ask small groups, pairs or individuals to role-play or mime something, and at certain points you stop the action by calling out 'Freeze!'

Ask the children to think of the character they want to be and to do the actions of that person. Throw in a challenge or a problem and the children can show their reactions to that situation in character. Stop the action and ask some to speak their thoughts (thought-tracking) as you tap them on the shoulder. Has anything changed? What happened to make them think like that? How will their character help solve the problem?

Follow up by reflecting on what happened and how they felt while in role.

● EXAMPLE ─────────────────────────────

Ask the class to imagine that they are in a shopping centre. Each pupil picks a character (e.g. shopper, security guard, cleaner, shopkeeper, parent or child) and then acts out what that character is doing. You can use thought-tracking to get the children to say what they are feeling in character. For example, the shopper might say, 'I must finish my shopping before I pick up my kids from school', while the security guard might say, 'Everything's quiet today, thank goodness.'

Now throw in a problem – for example, someone has stolen something from a shop and no one is allowed to leave the shopping centre until the truth has come out. How does each character feel? How will they get to the truth? Might there be a better way to solve this problem?

Freeze-frame and thought-tracking is best for:

- developing empathy

- understanding that different people have different reactions to situations

- developing problem-solving skills.

Role-play

This is probably the format everyone knows best, but although the term 'role-play' may strike fear into the heart of many adults, it's a great tool to use in PSHE lessons. Role-play works particularly well when pupils are given a scenario and can practise, develop and change their responses to it. Change the ending of the scenario and they have to respond to that change; encourage them to recognise how their words, body language and feelings change.

If you want some groups or pairs to show their scenarios to the class, it's usually best to warn them before they start the activity so that they have plenty of time to prepare. Younger children have a tendency to create role-plays of epic proportions, so if you want to be out of the classroom by midnight, use a timer to set a time limit on their magnum opus. While it's sometimes helpful for others to see their work, it has equal value when it's simply about the process.

● EXAMPLE ─────────────────────────────────

After some learning on the meanings of 'passive', 'aggressive' and 'assertive', give pairs a scenario to act out in which the characters want different things. Ask them to act it out three times: once with one person being *passive*, once with that person being *aggressive*, and once with the same person being *assertive*.

How did the other person react? How did that person's words and actions change? How did each person in the scenario feel?

Role-play is best for:

- developing and practising skills

- co-operation

- exploring feelings in a safe environment.

Conscience corridors

Divide the group or class into two equal parts. One group must think of all the persuasive arguments *for* a given position, and the other must think of the arguments *against*. Encourage the pupils to think of as many arguments for and against as possible. They could either work together in a group or individually.

The two opposing sides then form a corridor by standing in lines facing one another. Ask a confident pupil to walk through the corridor, or walk through it yourself. As you pass, one person from the 'For' side speaks and then one person from the 'Against' side speaks. The idea is to hear all the arguments one by one and then at the end of the corridor to decide which set of arguments has been the most persuasive. While it might sometimes seem counter-intuitive to encourage pupils to see both sides of an argument, this helps them to realise that issues are often complex and that in order to make key decisions they do need to know both sides of the story.

● EXAMPLE

As part of a lesson on making healthier choices, you ask the children to create a conscience corridor around the pros and cons of drinking sugary drinks. As you pass through the corridor, you might hear, 'You'll end up at the dentist more if you drink sugary drinks', and then 'What's the harm in having a can of fizzy pop every now and then?'

Which side has the strongest argument? Can pupils see why it's sometimes hard to make choices?

Conscience corridors are best for:

- consolidating and practising new skills

- seeing both sides of the argument

- developing problem-solving skills.

❋ SOMETHING TO THINK ABOUT

This is just a small selection of the drama techniques you can use in PSHE sessions. You may have your own tried-and-tested ideas.

Try planning a lesson that uses a technique that is new to you. Each technique here can be used with younger or older children, depending on what scenarios and stories you use. Younger children may need some adult input for the conscience corridor, but are still able to take part effectively.

Find out what works best for your class and share ideas with colleagues. Think about the point in a lesson or a series of lessons when a drama activity might have the greatest impact and when it could lead to further learning or a written activity.

Using more familiar techniques

As well as discussion and drama activities, the following tried-and-tested techniques can also help create a backbone to your outstanding PSHE lessons.

Making decisions

Activities could include 'True–False', 'Agree–Disagree' or 'Yes–No' positions. For example, children could stand on a continuum from 'Agree' to 'Disagree' (a 'confidence line'), or there could be four corners with pupils moving to the corner that best reflects their thinking (e.g. 'Strongly Agree'/'Agree'/'Disagree'/'Strongly Disagree'). Remind pupils that opinions may differ and that there may be more than one 'right' answer.

Another activity that focuses pupils' thinking is diamond nine ranking where pairs of small groups are given nine statements, facts or sentences about a topic on small squares of card or paper. Through discussion the pupils must rank the statements in order of priority, with one card at the top, two in the next row, then rows of three, two and one, forming a diamond shape.

Expressing an opinion or a thought

You could create a graffiti wall using large sheets of paper, or on-screen using tablets. Children are asked to write a sentence, a phrase or a word or to add their ideas. This is also good for checking understanding and learning.

Drawing and writing

Ask pupils to draw a picture or write a sentence in response to a question. This might be done individually or in a pair or a group. Think of activities like these:

- Draw a school playground where bullying happens. Now draw a playground where bullying never happens and describe the differences.

- Draw a healthy person.

- Design a toolkit for staying safe online.

- Fill the outline of a body with positive thoughts.

While it's fine to offer some sort of scaffolding in the form of a worksheet every now and then, try to avoid endless worksheets in PSHE.

Problem-solving

Create scenarios and set problems that pupils need to solve through discussion, drawing, writing or role-play. The problems may arise from the initial lesson stimulus or may be devised by the teacher. They could also be real-life problems that need solving in your school – 'How can we manage the playground equipment rota to ensure fairness?', 'How could we begin to sort out the littering problem in school?', 'How can we make sure that new pupils are helped to settle in?'

Playing games

Use tried-and-tested game formats or PSHE topics. Think of games like bingo (great for recapping topic information), Kim's game (where you secretly remove an object from a set of items and the children have to identify what has gone – good for reinforcing new vocabulary taught to the children), game-show formats, and sorting (which encourages talking and teamwork).

Creating and making

This can be making posters and leaflets (use this sparingly so that PSHE doesn't become an endless series of 'Make a poster about...' tasks), designing and presenting information and learning using IT, making a magazine or book cover, devising a game, taking a photograph, making a record or making a present.

Writing

Write a story, a poem, an advice guide, a list of instructions, a recipe, a paragraph or sentence, or a description. Or complete the sentence, annotate, describe and advise.

Be careful that the success criteria for the activities are always clear, and that the activity isn't about the colouring, decorating and making for its own sake. It's important that work in PSHE is presented to the same high standard as other subject areas, so ensure that learning is PSHE-related and not a time-filler.

Ending well

End the lesson with a plenary in which you recap the learning and review whether you have achieved the learning outcomes. You may have your own methods that work well with your class. This may include asking the children to share or feed back some of their learning, but try to avoid the whole class sharing what they've done – keep the focus on recapping learning or this could become a show-and-tell session. Finish with a game or look back at the initial question or challenge from the beginning of the lesson.

Send pupils off with something to think about, something to try out or a challenge or task to work on. Tell them when you'll be following up on the takeaway task. Then, over the following days, give them a chance to share their experiences. Examples could include:

- 'Try and do one extra kind thing per day for the rest of the week.'

- 'Try out your assertiveness skills in the playground.'

- 'This week, try one new food you wouldn't normally eat.'

- 'Keep an exercise diary for a week.'

- 'Note where the litter bins are in the local area and encourage your friends and family to use them.'

Introducing assessment

'Surely we don't need to assess PSHE? How do you assess feelings and emotions and abstract concepts? You can't have a test of those! We've just experienced a really fun, engaging lesson and now we have to stop and assess it! No, thanks.'

And yet if PSHE is to be taught well and with the rigour we allocate to other subject areas, we *must* assess learning and progress in PSHE. Assessment in PSHE is consistently judged to be weaker than in other areas. For example, the Ofsted report *Not Yet Good Enough*[1] found that:

> By far the weakest aspect of teaching was the assessment of pupils' learning which was often less robust for PSHE education than for other subjects. In too many schools, teachers did not check or build

---

1 Ofsted (2013) *Not Yet Good Enough: Personal, Social, Health and Economic Education in Schools – Personal Social and Health Education in English Schools in 2012*. London: Ofsted.

on pupils' previous knowledge which resulted in them repeating topics, and they had lower expectations of the quality of pupils' work in PSHE education than for the same pupils in other subjects.

Crucially the report observes that:

Where the curriculum was strong it built on pupils' previous knowledge both in PSHE education lessons and in other subjects.

Why do we need to assess PSHE? The answer lies with the same reasons we assess other subject areas in school: to find out where pupils are at now and what they need to learn, to identify the gaps in knowledge and understanding, to focus on what is learned rather than just what is taught, to help pupils identify their own learning needs and to ensure progression throughout the school. In PSHE in particular, assessment also helps to structure the spiral curriculum, to identify the current needs of pupils and to eliminate repetition. But assessment doesn't need to be onerous.

Assessment starts with planning. Your PSHE lesson plans should have learning objectives but perhaps more importantly success criteria. If you're using lesson plans that don't have success criteria, it's worth creating your own so that you have a clear understanding in your mind of exactly where children should be at the end of the session and whether they meet those success criteria or not. A learning objective about the impact of language and words could be:

- To reflect on the impact that words can have.

And expressed as a success criterion that might be:

- Pupils can describe some words that can hurt and kind words and phrases.

Break that down further and you may get:

- All pupils will be able to name five words that can be hurtful and five that can be kind.

- Some pupils will be able to describe in more detail how these words make us feel (empathy).

Assessment for Learning (AfL)

Before teaching starts we need to establish where children are with their learning, understanding and skills. One of the criticisms levelled at PSHE (particularly by pupils themselves) is that PSHE can be repetitive. There's no need for that repetition when there are so many areas of learning in PSHE. In Chapter Two we looked at the overlapping topic areas, synergy between them and where PSHE supports and consolidates learning. Before a module of learning is taught and before a new topic is tackled, it's important to find out exactly what the children know already, what they need to learn, what possible misconceptions they have and whether they have any burning questions that need answering. AfL will help uncover these so that you can pitch lessons correctly and ensure that these lessons are effective and address the needs of your pupils.

More formal AfL

One of the simplest ways of getting started with AfL is to start with a brief class discussion in which you introduce the new topic or area of learning. Then ask each child to draw a spider diagram with the topic at the centre. Ask them to add in questions they want answered and information they already know. Use a blank piece of paper or have a prepared sheet that pupils can stick into their book or put in a folder. Use prompts like 'Things I'd like to know about [the topic]', 'Things I know about [the topic]' and 'Three questions I'd like to ask about [the topic]'. For younger pupils, make the sheet simpler, with perhaps one question, or ask them to draw some of the things they know. If for example the new topic is about keeping healthy, ask pupils to draw as many things that keep us healthy as possible. You could offer a sheet divided into squares and ask pupils to draw a new suggestion in each box. After the topic you can revisit the sheets and ask pupils to add in their new information, skills and answers to questions using a different-coloured pen or pencil. A range of pre-prepared sheets with boxes or shapes will help. This can also be done as a whole class or in groups with additional adult help. Use flipchart paper and create a class diagram about what we know now and what we want to find out. You can then introduce the topic and talk about questions and areas of interest you will be addressing in PSHE, and how.

Using the suggested discussion techniques outlined earlier in this chapter, give each group a question about a new topic and ask them to write notes or have a scribe jot down some notes and ideas. Pool the notes at the end and discuss them as a group or class. Identify any gaps in learning and how you will address these in the topic.

Created as a piece of research into drugs by Southampton University in the 1970s, the 'Jugs and Herrings' (a child's misunderstanding of the phrase 'drugs and heroin') 'draw and write' technique has passed into PSHE lore. Designed to establish understanding before teaching a module on drug education, it can be adapted for other topic areas. The original 'draw and write' exercise starts with pupils working on their own. Working on a piece of paper folded into sections, the pupils follow as the teacher tells a story about two children who are walking home and find a bag of drugs. In the first box the children are asked to draw what was in the bag of drugs. The story continues and the teacher is then able to see exactly what the children understand about and around drugs. It's worth remembering that even though children may be of similar ages and from similar backgrounds, their knowledge and understanding may be very diverse. You'll need to think about how your planned lessons address the needs of all the children in your class. 'Draw and write' can be simplified for younger pupils, and because it is about drawing (the 'write' bit comes in as children are invited to annotate their drawings if they wish), it is more accessible than written activities.

Try graffiti sheets, where you write a question on a large sheet of paper and pupils can write their thoughts, ideas and suggestions on the paper or stick on Post-it® notes.

Confidence lines and RAG ratings can be useful starting points. Write or ask a question or statement and ask pupils to give themselves a rating of one to five or red, amber or green. Keep questions clear and specific to try to avoid children overestimating their prior knowledge. A clear statement might be 'I can name five different things I can do to keep safe online' rather than 'I know how to stay safe online'.

Formal questionnaires and surveys also have a place, but assessment is not always about reams of paper with quantifiable results for every topic. The aim is to find out where children are now and to be able to measure progress in learning in a way that is appropriate to the topic and that adds value to learning.

Less formal AfL

Assessment should be an integral part of every PSHE lesson. While formal AfL at the beginning of a topic or module helps to tailor learning to the needs of your class, each session should start with a warm-up or starter activity that also incorporates a chance for the teacher to observe how pupils interact with what they already know and to garner an idea of their understanding and attitudes.

So a starting activity needs to reflect the content of the lesson to come. Starter activities like 'Agree/Disagree' corners, problem-solving games and teamwork games will help set the scene. Take a corners game, for example. Label each corner 'Strongly agree', 'Agree', 'Disagree' and 'Strongly disagree', or just 'Agree' and 'Disagree' for younger children. Pose a question and get children moving to the corner that best fits their answer. This gets the children moving and sets them off thinking about the topic in hand. As the teacher you'll gain an idea of what the children know already, which areas they're struggling with or where they lack understanding. Where are the gaps in learning or understanding? Any attitudes that need addressing? Before getting started on the main section of the lesson, you already have a better understanding of class and individual need.

When planning lessons, try to build in AfL and you'll find the sessions will be more meaningful to the pupils and more likely to address the success criteria.

Assessment of Learning (AoL)

Using the success criteria for your lesson, you'll know exactly what needs assessing after the lesson or set of lessons. It's now a case of matching the best assessment method to the success criteria to help you find out whether learning took place and whether progress in learning and understanding has happened as planned.

As with AfL, formal methods can include questionnaires, surveys and written methods. Ask children to draw, write or create a formal end product that demonstrates their learning. This could be an end product used for display, written work, diagrams, or a self-assessment or peer assessment.

Less formally, AoL can also be built into the lesson activities themselves. For example, when hot-seating you can observe and assess what sorts of questions are being asked and how the respondent responds; observing the response to the speed-dating problem-solving activity can give you an understanding of how pupils select advice and support, the quality of the advice and how this reflects learning content; and a drawing of a toolkit for bereavement and loss will help demonstrate whether the pupil has understood what a bereaved person may need in terms of emotional support. The activity and assessment are integrated and not separate entities.

Self-assessment

The following method of self-assessment is useful for Key Stage 2 pupils where you want to encourage them to really reflect on what they've learnt. After a PSHE lesson or a series of lessons, give each pupil a slip of paper or Post-it® note. In pairs or preferably individually (pupils may need help until they get used to the method), ask pupils to reflect on what they've learnt in the session and write on the slip of paper:

- 'I know...'

- 'I can...'

- 'I understand...'

It's an important part of the session and pupils should be able to describe what skills they have after each session. For example, after a lesson on conflict management, a child might write:

- 'I know you have to listen to both sides when there is a problem.'

- 'I can suggest ways of sorting out problems.'

- 'I understand that my ideas don't always work and that's okay!'

It may take some pupils some time to reflect and describe what they have learnt, so ask prompt questions like these:

- 'What can you do now that you couldn't do before?'

- 'What did you find out about in this activity?'

- 'How can you use some of the things you've learnt this week in school or at home?'

If you use this method on a regular basis or for a whole module, ask pupils to put their named and completed slips of paper in a box or jar (call it the 'I can' can) so you can have a read after the lesson. At the end of the module the children will have a small collection of slips of paper which they can then stick onto a larger sheet of paper as a record and an aide-mémoire of the skills they've developed. You can also see the progress from the first session to the last.

With younger children just use 'I can…' and ask pupils to draw, write or tell you one thing they can do now that they couldn't do before the lesson (e.g. 'I can tell the difference between hurtful and kind words'). Talk about what this might look like in day-to-day life ('I will try to use kind words more than hurtful words in class and in the playground') and the new skills the children have developed.

● CASE STUDY

I started using the 'I can' can with a group of Year Six girls. We meet on a weekly basis to develop and explore topics like conflict management, friendship and managing risk. When planning the lessons I made the success criteria match the pupils' development and what the head teacher wanted the group to learn. Each session finished with five minutes of writing their 'I can' statements. At first they needed a bit of help but by week three had a really good understanding of how to express their learning and enjoyed adding little decorations to their statements too. At the end of the six-week module I stuck their slips of paper on a sheet and handed them out. The girls really enjoyed reading their own answers and could clearly see how much they had learned over the course of a few weeks. It was also a useful record for their class teachers so they could refer to the skills they knew the girls had explored and a good way of showing progress. The class teachers knew exactly what topics needed to be tackled or revisited next.

PSHE adviser

Need some more ideas? Table 4.1 sets out a variety of ways of assessing PSHE, linked to some of those planned activities.

Table 4.1 Assessing PSHE

	Assessment for Learning (AfL)	Assessment of Learning (AoL)
Four corners: 'Agree/Disagree'; 'True/False'; 'Yes/No'	Find out what pupils know already and where the gaps are. Are there any misconceptions?	How have children made progress? Have they retained the knowledge and can they demonstrate their skills in critical thinking? Have there been any changes of attitude? Any areas that still need addressing?
Diamond nines	Where is their thinking right now? What do children know already, and what do they need to know or understand?	Has thinking changed in the light of learning? Can children give a rationale for their answers?
Draw and write	What understanding do pupils have of the topic? What is the breadth of their knowledge and understanding?	How do children demonstrate their learning now? Any misconceptions?
Scenarios and problem-solving	As a whole-class or group exercise, what do children know now?	Can children now tackle simple problem-solving on their own or in pairs? Do they know where to go if they need support?
Graffiti boards/ Post-it® notes	Where are pupils now? What is their thinking?	How have children made progress? Compare their thinking before and after.
'Radio/TV' interviews	What is a pupils' take on the topic? What do they need to find out?	Can they describe what they found out and how they went about it?
Sentence starters	In a round or as circle time, give a sentence starter and find out what children know already.	What do children know now? Check their skills and understanding.
Games including bingo and TV-style games	Any questions that children can't answer? Where is their learning at the moment?	Have gaps in learning been covered? Can pupils express their understanding?
Team challenges/ games	Any flashpoints or difficulties? How do pupils solve the problem?	Can pupils use problem-solving skills and appropriate language in solving team problems?
Photo or film-clip stimulus	Can pupils describe what they saw, how the characters felt, and why characters acted as they did?	Have pupils developed their vocabulary? Have they developed skills such as empathy and critical thinking?

Recording and evidence

How much you record, what sort of evidence you collect and what you do with it will depend on your school, but instigating some sort of recording system will help raise the profile of assessment. Consider having a formal assessment at set points in the programme – at the end of a module or set of lessons, or half-termly. While it's important to have assessment opportunities in all PSHE lessons, there may be a range of types of evidence in written, verbal and recorded learning. Decide what evidence you need to keep and how this shows pupil progress in PSHE. This should reflect the learning that has gone on in the lessons and acts as a checkpoint for where pupils have got to, how much they remember and can apply, and what steps they need to take next.

If you've used, for example, the 'I know, I can, I understand' idea, you'll end up with a sheet with a set of slips for each child. Children could then write a short self-assessment reflecting on how they have used the skills they've learnt and how they plan to use them. Younger children could describe their learning to an adult, complete a confidence line or emoji chart, or record their reflections verbally using a recording app or device. Evidence can also be collected by using an online bulletin board like Padlet.

You may decide to have a book or folder in which to collect examples and evidence; or these could be photographed and collected virtually, and could then be shared with the next class teacher to provide a clear line of progress throughout the school. Schemes and resources often have their own assessment and recording sheets. Think carefully about how often you want to use these methods of assessment, what they add to the children's learning and how they support your teaching.

As part of this process of assessment you might want to think about how you report to parents. This may be done as part of the personal profile in the annual report, where you can refer to which specific topics the child has covered, the skills they have developed and the progress they made throughout the year – how they have contributed to discussion, shown their understanding of new skills, put these skills into practice, and developed their understanding and critical thinking – and what they need to do next.

❋ SOMETHING TO THINK ABOUT

Look at your PSHE lesson plan and identify where assessment is happening. Use a highlighter to highlight opportunities and begin to add in assessment activities into the body of the lessons. Consider how the evidence impacts on future PSHE learning.

Chapter Five

BEYOND THE PSHE CURRICULUM

In order for PSHE to be truly meaningful and make a real difference it has to be fully embedded across the school, and that doesn't just mean the lessons in which PSHE is taught. The messages need to be consistently applied across the whole school community, and closely linked to SMSC and the school ethos. So in order to bring PSHE to life even more and to truly wave the PSHE flag, there are some added extras you can unlock.

Thinking about circle time

Circle time is one way of delivering PSHE and facilitating discussion, but in itself it is not PSHE. When planned well, circle time can be effective as a forum for discussing issues in a whole class setting, but despite appearances it takes time to set up and run well. Think carefully about whether circle time is the best way of delivering your PSHE objectives and outcomes or whether there may be another way. As a way of starting a discussion or as part of a PSHE session, circle time has a real value when used carefully and sparingly. It is a tool that facilitates learning not only in PSHE but in other subject areas too, but it should never take the place of well-planned PSHE teaching and learning.

The idea of circle time is – as the name suggests – that the class sits in a circle and each member of the circle in turn gives their ideas, thoughts and feelings when holding an item that allows them to speak. This needs to be done with a set of rules (who can speak and when, how to listen and sit attentively, etc.). Circle time works well when the teacher poses a question and each pupil gives their answers or thoughts. Pupils are allowed to pass when it's their turn, but in practice most children opt to say something. This means that the whole group can hear what each person is thinking and what they have to say, but one of the drawbacks of circle time is that it can feel slow and repetitive. Younger children in particular sometimes do their thinking when it's their turn, so circle time is punctuated by silence. The teacher then steps in to encourage or hurry the child as the rest of the circle starts to get fidgety.

If you want to use circle time in your classroom then it's important to spend some time establishing the circle-time rules and having circle-time materials ready, including a speaking item, rules on card or in visual form, objects and simple games. Circle time may be used in reacting to an issue arising in school or beyond, but it should be focused and should have an intended outcome, just like any other well-planned PSHE session.

Using some of the suggestions in the section on consulting with children, ask the pupils who take part in circle time whether they feel that it is valuable as a learning resource, and what works well and doesn't work so well. If you want to plan circle-time activities into your curriculum then read up on what works, how to deliver it and good practice techniques. Jenny Mosley has developed her Quality Circle Time method, and her website has everything you need to know about circle time and whether it's for you and your school.

❋ SOMETHING TO THINK ABOUT

Read up a bit more about circle time and consider whether it's a method of delivery that might work for you and your classroom. If you've not taught with circle time before, perhaps have a go at leading a session and reflect on whether it works for you and your pupils. If you use circle time on a regular basis, consider whether there are other methods of teaching that could be more effective. For more information, read more about Jenny Mosley's circle-time method: www.circle-time.co.uk.

Encouraging pupil voice

Done well, pupil voice can be a helpful addition to the PSHE curriculum and can provide a way of seeking pupils' views on a range of school matters. Like all areas of PSHE, however, it needs to build on need and be embedded in the fabric of the school. Perhaps you have a school council that meets every now and then and discusses various topics of concern, and perhaps this is run separately from the PSHE curriculum, possibly by a different teacher. Perhaps it's time for a shake-up of how you use pupil voice in your school.

The first question is: what do we want to achieve? What do teaching and non-teaching staff know about the school council and its role? What do pupils in all years know about the school council and how they can contribute to it? How are councillors picked and what are their roles? Does the contact teacher lead the meetings and direct the discussion or is it fully led by pupils? How do we make pupil voice meaningful?

A study conducted in 2007[1] found that the most successful school councils were the ones that had a clear rationale for introducing pupil voice. School councils may have become lost in the processes rather than the purpose of pupil voice, and may not be the best method for enabling pupil voice.

Consider the *whys* of having a school council before the *hows*. There may be a particular focus for pupil voice, such as seeking input into a new behaviour management system or planning a charity fundraiser, rather than unfocused general complaints. School council should not be a time where pupils complain about the niggles and then pass them on to the adults to sort out. It's better to encourage pupils to be fully proactive in driving a project forward, and to influence and create change, rather than to report on toilets and playground arguments. (These are important, of course, but may be better solved in other ways.) Think of projects like choosing, setting up and running charity events; promoting better teamwork across the school and between year groups; setting up and running paired reading schemes; planning and running playground schemes, including budgeting for and ordering equipment; running a peer mentoring scheme; or leading the school travel plan.

---

1   Whitty, G. and Wisby, E. (2007) *Real Decision Making? School Councils in Action.* London: Institute of Education, University of London.

In terms of electing members, think about how this will be done and how often they will change. Who will train these councillors? How do you ensure equality of opportunity, or is it a popularity contest in which the most articulate and vocal pupils are elected time and again? Do you teach the democratic process across the school before the elections happen so that the process is placed in context? How can you have a robust system of communication between all pupils and their elected representatives? Are children's voices genuinely being heard?

Pupil voice need not be limited to the school council. Consider other pupil action groups working on particular projects and focus groups helping to shape the curriculum – sports, arts, environment and the travel plan, for example. Pupil voice is found through surveys and questionnaires, through class work including PSHE lessons, through school ambassadors, monitors and prefects, and through focus groups and hands-up surveys.

Think about how you will monitor the impact of pupil voice and how you will communicate any changes to pupils. As adults we know how frustrating it is when our opinion is sought but then not acted upon, with no justification given!

Making visits and inviting visitors

Visits and visitors can really bring learning in PSHE alive, and they don't have to break the bank. Look at your planned programme of PSHE and consider where and how visitors could support learning and which elements of PSHE you could bring out through visits.

If you invite a visitor into your school or classroom, this must be in order to enhance the curriculum. Consider what skills or attributes they bring that will support your curriculum but add a little more expertise. Visitors should never be a substitute for planned PSHE but should support and enhance it. It's easy to feel relieved if a visitor offers to deliver part of the RSE programme or a drugs and alcohol workshop, but remember that these are only one part of the whole programme. No visitor can ever replace a well-planned programme of learning that addresses the needs of *your* pupils in *your* school setting. So here is a list of some suggested visitors who may be able to add value.

Theatre companies

Theatre companies offering Theatre in Education (TIE) programmes can really help to bring the curriculum alive. They often plan tours and might contact your school direct to offer you a visit. You may also have local tried-and-tested companies. A well-produced TIE experience can help pupils make sense of a particular topic, and experienced companies will also offer pupil evaluations and perhaps a workshop as well. Some offer parental support and teacher training too, as part of their package. These visits don't come cheap, but when you consider what they offer they often represent good value for money. Perhaps think about fitting a TIE visit in with a themed week or consider asking the PTA to help fundraise.

Checklist

Ask the company for references. A good TIE company will have references and testimonials from other schools they've worked with. They will have consulted with schools and specialists during the research and development phase of the play and will have taken feedback on board. If they're in the local area, ask if you can see a show: that way you'll know exactly what they offer. If not, the company will often have short video clips you can watch and they'll be happy to chat to you about your school's needs. If you're still not sure, get in contact with a school that has already had the show and ask them how it added value to their PSHE curriculum.

On the day of the visit, make sure the space is ready for the TIE company. They run to a tight schedule, so if a hall that is supposed to be available for 8.30 a.m. is being used for assembly, then this will affect the timings of the performance. Check health and safety needs and if possible make sure the company has a small space in which to change and prepare. Don't forget water, tea and coffee. Always make sure there are plenty of adults supporting children during the show – it's part of the teaching and learning curriculum, so staff need to attend in order to get the most out of the show. After the visit, ask for feedback and any teaching resources they have that complement the show.

Charities and other providers

Charities and other providers may offer to deliver workshops based on their topic and these will often have a fundraising element to them.

The larger charities often have excellent resource materials that support learning in the classroom. Decide whether the charity is right for your school and how you will communicate this to the whole school community. It's hard to say no to a charity, but it may be easier to set your school's supported charities at the beginning of the school year. Make sure learning is linked to the planned PSHE curriculum, so that it's not a bolt-on.

Checklist

Do some research on your chosen charity or speaker. Make sure you understand fully what they will be talking about with your children, and if necessary check references. Some charities will have a very particular slant – if so, make sure this chimes with the ethos of your school. Make sure you speak with the person who will be delivering the workshops and find out whether they need any specialist equipment. Prepare the children for the visit so that they know and understand a little about the charity beforehand.

Local community members

Local community members may include those from the emergency services, those in the council, or local democracy, faith or community leaders. It's good to place the school in the context of the local community in which the children live, so these visits can be really helpful. Again, though, these visits should not replace the planned curriculum. For example, the local community police may be able to help with talking to children about personal safety, safe travel or drugs and alcohol, but these talks are to support the curriculum, not to replace it. They may address one aspect within a module of learning. Explore local democracy by talking to council officers, local councillors or your local member of parliament. You may need to think well in advance!

Checklist

Think about where in the school year you may want to have a talk or a visit from local community members. It's best if you give them plenty of advance warning and get a date in the diary at the beginning of the school year, so that you can plan the curriculum accordingly. If your local community police officer has delivered 'stranger danger' for many years, then think about whether they can support you in other ways. Perhaps you could have a 'stranger danger' talk every other year and a 'safe travel' visit for Years Five and Six instead. Could you link this to road safety week, walking to school, or the transition to secondary school?

Health professionals

You may be lucky enough to have a school nurse who can help with delivering PSHE. However, many are now so busy with individual case work that their time is very limited. It's definitely worth asking whether the school nurse can help with key topics that may need health expertise, such as aspects of RSE and talking about vaccinations. Again, their contribution is not to replace your own teaching of RSE but they may be able to complement and support learning. Work together to support each other in delivering topics – your school nurse has medical expertise but is not necessarily a teacher, and vice versa: together you may be able to deliver a stronger session! Ask a local pharmacist if they'd be willing to visit to chat about safety in medicines and keeping healthy, and perhaps you have a dentist who could talk about dental health.

Checklist

The key to effective work with a health professional is good communication. Get dates in the diary early and make sure you explain exactly what you need from them and how you will support them in class. Prepare the class beforehand and follow up with planned activities. Health professionals can also help with signposting to further support for families, so make sure you let parents know their contact details and about specialist services they offer.

Parents

You have an amazing resource right at your fingertips in the form of parents and carers! Invite parents with PSHE-related jobs to deliver a talk or a presentation or simply to take part in a question-and-answer session. Think about holding a job fair, where parents talk about their working lives and share some insights into their jobs and the skills they use day to day. Parents with babies may be good visitors for children learning about how we grow or what babies need in order to thrive.

Checklist

If you're not used to talking to a large group of inquisitive children this can be pretty daunting, so make sure parents who visit know that you will be there to support them every step of the way. Give them an idea of the sort of questions the children will ask, or structure the talk as a question-and-answer session which puts you in control of the session. Remind the parent to bring in equipment, items or photographs that can illustrate their talk and bring it to life.

If you're going to arrange visits into school, it's helpful to have a visitor policy so that everyone knows their role. The following checklist may help.

● CHECKLIST: HOSTING VISITORS

Before the visit

- Check references and find out more about the prospective visitor. Check that what they offer is right for your pupils and that it will add value to your PSHE curriculum.

- Let parents know that the visitor is coming, so that they can chat to their child about the visit both before it happens and afterwards.

- Ensure that you have the right space for the visitor, whether that's the hall, a classroom or an outdoor space. Check that the visit is in the school diary and make sure you haven't been double-booked. If something comes up that would affect the visit, let the visitor know as soon as possible.

- Ask the visitor about their travel arrangements and whether they need a space to park (do you need to provide a parking permit?), advice about public transport or contact details for a taxi from the station.

- Make sure the visit is a planned part of the PSHE programme. Ensure that pupils know in advance about the visitor and are ready to learn, and that they understand what they are learning and why they are learning it.

Remind them of behaviour rules and make sure you are always in the classroom to support the visitor.

- If it's a theatre company or a visitor with specialist equipment, make a health and safety assessment. Make sure visitors understand the safety rules of the school.

- Let them know of any special requirements of pupils. Reassure them that you won't leave them alone with the children at any time.

- If you want to take photos, check that the visitor is happy with this. If the visitor wants to take photos, ensure that you have permission and that the visitor understands where these photos may be used.

On the day

- Make sure the reception desk staff know what time the visitor is arriving and who they are. It's embarrassing for the visitor if they turn up at the office and no one knows about their visit!

- Once the visitor has arrived, don't leave them sitting in the reception area for ages. Make sure they sign in. Check that they know where the loos are and have been offered a drink. (It might sound obvious, but this can often be overlooked on a busy day.) Is there somewhere safe they can leave their belongings?

- Make sure they know where to access your school's child protection procedures (some schools offer a small card or leaflet to visitors). Check that they understand their responsibilities to the pupils – not to be alone with them; to work with the teacher in terms of behaviour management; and to use language and content appropriate to the age group.

- Check that the space is ready and that pupils are ready to listen.

- Barring any major problems, make sure you stick to the timetable for the visit. Enjoy the visit!

- Thank the visitor. Ensure that they sign out and get to their transport.

After the visit

- Check that pupils understood what they were learning. Make sure that you follow up, for example with additional learning or signposting to further support.

- Ask pupils for feedback regarding the visit and what they learnt.

- Always write a 'thank you' letter or email to the visitor.

- If the visit was a success, ask the visitor to pencil in a date for another visit.

- Give the visitor feedback about their visit and what the pupils got out of it. What worked, what could have gone even better, and what would you do differently next time?

You'll have lots of additional ideas for visits and visitors. You could liaise with neighbouring schools to find out whom they recommend or to pair up to buy in theatre companies. Think creatively and enjoy bringing the PSHE curriculum to life!

Planning a theme day or week

Running a PSHE-themed day or week is one way of raising the profile of PSHE in your school and covering a topic in depth. Focusing on a particular area – such as Science and PSHE, healthy lifestyles, careers or money – can also help focus the whole school community on a particular area of learning. In the chapter on planning PSHE we looked at the different ways PSHE can be planned into the curriculum, and a themed day or week can add value if time is at a premium in a particular term or year.

PSHE can be a single focus or a joint one. It's a natural fit with Science and PE, but it can also feed into Book Week or World Book Day. It finds a natural home in linked campaigns like an anti-bullying week, World Mental Health Day or a road-safety awareness week. Check the PSHE Association calendar of events for comprehensive links throughout the year.

If you're planning a theme day or week, then the following checklist will help with planning and may provide some starting points.

● CHECKLIST: PLANNING A THEME DAY OR WEEK

General

- Is there a theme?

- What is your overarching aim? What do you want the pupils to get out of the week/day? Will there be an end product or a celebration event?

- What's in the budget?

- How much of the timetable will be related to the theme? (All of it, afternoons, breaks and lunchtimes, or occasional activities?)

- Who is going to help? (Parents, staff, governors, outside agencies, caterers, local businesses?)

- Is there a timetable for staff to help with planning and delivery?

- How will families be involved? (Parent workshops? A parent forum?)

- How will you promote the day/week and celebrate successes? (Via the school website, local links, in the press?)

- Consider the shape of the week/day (e.g. launch, daily challenge, demos, talks, competitions, carousel activities, celebration event).

- Who will deliver what, and do they know their responsibilities?

Possibilities

- *Free or low-cost talks and activities:* Local community members, parents, or representatives of agencies linked to the school (e.g. a police officer, a nurse, a pharmacist, a specialist teacher, someone from a local business, a charity or the local gym).

- *Paid activities:* Theatre in Education programmes, trips out, specialist workshops, workshops for parents, sports activities.

- *Information:* A resource pack for families?

- *Event:* Health afternoon, presentation, exhibition, school picnic, meal, show or celebration.

- *Funding:* Sponsored event to raise money for charity or to cover some of the costs (e.g. run, danceathon, cooking, dressing up, a challenge).

- *Topics:* Emotional health and wellbeing (e.g. anti-bullying, friendships, working together, team bonding, life skills, growing up, transitions, the playground, body image, media).

- *Staff:* What about staff wellbeing?

The key questions in running a theme day or week are: What will the impact be? How does this add to children's PSHE learning? It makes sense to have one point of contact for a theme week, but be sure there's room to delegate and ask for help. Enlist a link governor and a parent or carer and additional colleagues to help, or the burden may get heavy very quickly and be piled on top of everything else.

With the above in mind, start by brainstorming ideas for the following topics (as a working party, or as a whole staff group if you have some time in a staff meeting):

- Involving parents and the wider community.

- Ideas for activities and possible costs (£, ££ or £££).

- Monitoring impact and benefit.

- Who could help (planning and delivering).

- Supporting and involving vulnerable pupils or groups of pupils (such as pupils with SEND, young carers, or new arrivals).

Ask staff to try and be creative in their thinking – at this stage it's about gathering a broad selection of ideas. While it's nice to be ambitious, try also to think about what can realistically be achieved. Running this activity once with some teachers, one wrote down: 'Invite Jamie Oliver to come and do a cooking workshop.' If only it were that easy! But if Mr Oliver may not be able to pop in to deliver free workshops, how could you access expertise from other sources? A representative from the catering company? A local chef? Someone from the catering department of a Further Education college? Or maybe a member of staff or parent who is a keen cook or baker?

Theme days or weeks offer an opportunity to get parents and carers involved in a broader way in the life of the school, and they can help to encourage parents who don't usually get involved. Consider running a parent forum, where parents with jobs or skills talk about their work, bring in artefacts and answer questions. If you're taking a 'healthy lifestyles' approach, for example, find parents who work in health-related professions – hairdressers (the importance of keeping hair clean); cooks, food-preparation workers or waiting staff (healthy eating, hygiene in the workplace); carers (physical and emotional care); or street cleaners (keeping the environment clean and healthy). If you have surgeons, athletes and celebrity chefs that's great too, but think creatively.

Encourage governors and school community members such as faith leaders, volunteers or club leaders to share any work or hobby experiences. Perhaps you have a ballroom-dancing governor or a footballing faith leader, or a club leader who runs dance classes as well as children's clubs.

You might want to present the parent skills as a question-and-answer session, as this takes the pressure off the parent in having to come up with a 'talk' or 'presentation'. Keep it informal and chatty (think genial chat-show host) and reassure them the children will enjoy it. It can be daunting facing a room full of children if you're not used to it, even for experienced and confident parents. Make sure invited parents know the child-protection procedures and make them welcome as a special guest in school. Afterwards write a letter, card or email of thanks.

The following questions can help get the ball rolling:

- What is your job title and where do you work?

- What is your average working day like?

- What are the most important parts of the job?

- What do you enjoy about it most? And least?

- How did you get into this job?

- What helps you do your job?

- Do you have to wear a uniform or special clothes?

- What advice would you give someone who wanted to do the same job as you?

Consider running parent workshops either for parents alone or with their children. They could be related to a topic such as internet safety, mindfulness, cooking healthier meals, packing a healthier lunchbox, trying a new sport or activity, or first-aid basics.

Think about holding a sponsored event or fundraiser for charity, or to raise funds for a related need such as sports or Science equipment. Simple sponsored events could be dressing-up days (e.g. dress as your favourite scientist or sports personality), a sponsored run (different lengths, depending on age), a healthy snack sale (think twice about a bake sale if your event is about healthy lifestyles – while it's a definite crowd-pleaser and fundraiser, a bake sale may give mixed messages during a health-themed week), a disco, a dance or a skipathon.

Think about activities to send home for families to enjoy together – a 'try something new every day' challenge (eat a new vegetable, try a new sport, go for a family walk, learn a new skill, etc.), a research or making project, or a diary activity – and award stickers and certificates for those who complete the challenges. For those children who may not have the opportunity to work on a home activity, offer time and space in the day to complete the challenges (e.g. drop-in lunchtime sessions) with friends, staff members or PTA support.

Start the day with whole-school or year-group exercises or dancing (if you don't already) and think about using every minute in the day for extra activities like lunchtime drop-in sessions, break-time mindfulness, before- and after-school activities, and maybe an evening event such as a barbeque or games evening. Enlist the support of a local supermarket to hold a healthy drop-in breakfast where all the children have the opportunity to share breakfast and play games together before school.

A celebration at the end of the week can help focus the whole school on a shared goal. This could be a picnic, a celebratory meal, a show, an exhibition, a fair or a television-format competition. Encourage all classes to contribute their learning and their achievements from the week.

Assess the week's impact through built-in activities like graffiti walls, diaries, journals, pupil focus groups, surveys, questionnaires (pupils and parents) and quizzes. Share the information with the whole school community and make sure the next steps in learning build upon this evidence. Set up computers and tablets with an online survey that pupils and adults can do when they're in school.

A PSHE-themed or health week takes a bit of planning, but the rewards can be huge. Assess the week for genuine impact and ensure that learning from the health week is consistently carried on throughout the school year. Activities that worked well and were popular during the week can be embedded in the normal school day.

Thinking about staff wellbeing

We can't talk about pupil health and wellbeing without mentioning staff wellbeing too. The teaching profession has undergone huge changes in the last 20 years, with more accountability, paperwork and a broad range of pupil ability and experience in our schools. While it's up to schools to impose policies on planning, marking and assessment, senior leaders still need to have evidence of progress, attainment and impact for all groups within school, so the pressures can seem never-ending.

It's no wonder, then, that PSHE sometimes gets short shrift in the hustle and bustle of the crowded curriculum, but previous sections in this book have talked about the importance of putting well-planned PSHE at the heart of the curriculum and how doing so could be one way of beginning to tackle some of the other areas related to behaviour, mental health and emotional literacy.

What good is it to have articulate, vocabulary-rich children with access to support in schools if the teachers are mentally exhausted? As a start, governing bodies and head teachers must ensure that teachers have time to plan, that they receive adequate breaks and that they have 'the time required to pursue their personal interests outside work'.[2] The teaching workload never feels finished and it can often feel as though you're only just keeping your head above water. Working longer hours is not always the solution, however, and it's essential that you don't neglect your own family, relationships and relaxation time. Make sure you take the time to play sport, hang out with friends, weave baskets, bake bread or jump around in the mosh pit as you listen to your favourite rock band. Make sure you get enough sleep and, if you really feel you've not put the hours in, get up a little earlier to finish rather than tapping away at the keyboard until the early hours.

Of course all this is easier said than done, but it's good to practise what you teach too. Safeguarding your own mental and physical health is crucial in order to be the best teacher you can be. If you ever feel overwhelmed or anxious, then get support before things get worse. If it's a professional concern, ask colleagues and your Senior Leadership Team (SLT) for support, talk to other colleagues via social media (like #ukedchat, #sltchat, #ukpastoralchat or #primaryrocks), and meet other colleagues through CPD, network meetings, Pedagoo (www.pedagoo.org) or Teachmeets (http://teachmeet.pbworks.com). There are also a range of local and national events created by teachers and for teachers, such as #WomenEd (www.womened.org), which connects women leaders and aspirational leaders in education (many of the workshops at their events are wellbeing-driven), #BAMEed (http://bameednetwork.com), which supports a range of diverse education leaders, and researchED (https://researched.org.uk).

There are many more. It's important to network with colleagues from other schools, to share problems and to explore new ways of working. No teacher is an island! In training evaluations and feedback, one of the things that is always mentioned is the opportunity to take some rare time out of the busy working day to network and chat with other teachers. On Twitter, join in with #teacher5aday for ideas on how to manage wellbeing moments during the school term and during the holidays. You don't even have to post on Twitter in order to read tweets and be inspired.

---

2   Department for Education (DfE) (2017) *School Teachers' Pay and Conditions: Guidance to Help Schools and Governing Bodies Develop their Approach to Teachers' and School Leaders' Pay*. London: DfE.

Integrate exercise into your working week, whether it's walking the dog, going to the gym, a quick cycle or a class. Try to eat healthily (some of the time at least!) and take time to sit when eating. There are always times when we need to be in the classroom with a staple gun in one hand and a sandwich in the other, but a few minutes' break won't hurt and might give you the headspace to face the afternoon. Occasionally take a walk around the local area at lunchtime, just to clear your head and have some fresh air. Although it's tempting to chug a sugar-laden fizzy drink or energy drink during the school day, be aware that these only give you a temporary release of energy before the post-sugar crash comes. Better to have a stash of energy-boosting snacks in school, like dried fruit and nuts (if these are allowed in school), yoghurt, fruit, toast or cereal, for low-sugar times or when you need an extra boost at staff meetings.

It's hard to get away from school issues when you're tied to a mobile phone, but try to have a cut-off point in the evening for school-related messages. Change the settings on your phone so that emails don't come in after a certain time so that family mealtimes or your relaxation time aren't ruined by a grumpy email that could have waited until morning but will now have you tossing and turning all night long with worry.

Consider adding a relaxation technique like mindfulness to your daily routine. Most teachers will be yelling 'I don't have time!', but even mindfulness or meditation need only take a few minutes and practising before bedtime may lead to better sleep. Try an app that fits in with your lifestyle.

Singing has proven health benefits, such as helping with breathing, lowering blood pressure and releasing tension, so join a choir and sing away the stress.[3] Other creative endeavours have also been shown to be good for emotional and physical health, so explore art, dance, drama, drawing, pottery or whatever else you're interested in. If you can't bear not to focus on school work then write a school play, create a game for use in class or design a greeting card, and don't forget to incorporate new passions and interests into your PSHE teaching.

Some schools have introduced wellbeing sessions as part of Inset or have developed 'random acts of kindness' or 'secret angels'. If the

---

3   For examples, see the website of the National Alliance for Arts, Health and Wellbeing: www.artshealthandwellbeing.org.uk.

workplace feels more friendly and supportive, then it's a happier place to work and all feel supported.

Above all, take a tip from PSHE practice and be assertive. If you really can't take anything else on or if you need to leave school at a certain time, then calmly and clearly state what you need. Try not to play the teacher-martyr and then whinge about your workload, colleagues or SLT (which can be passive-aggressive), or to get angry and aggressive with others. If you need time to think about a problem or request, ask for time to think and respond calmly with a reasoned argument and a suggestion for how that problem might be overcome or the request addressed.

If you're struggling, then make sure you ask for help before the problem becomes too big. Ask for help in school or seek advice from a union or from the Education Support Partnership (www.educationsupportpartnership.org.uk). Ask a colleague for moral support and talk to someone you can trust. Don't struggle on alone.

● CASE STUDY

At my previous schools I didn't have the confidence to say no to anything and I wasn't very good at delegating. By the end of summer term I was totally burnt out. I was grumpy and teary in school and definitely wasn't my best self for my class, which wasn't fair on them. When I started a new job as deputy head I made it very clear that I would be there for my pupils and my colleagues but that I would be leaving school straight after Monday's staff meeting (any follow-up could wait until the next day) and that on Wednesdays I had an exercise class to go to that I enjoyed. I'd get changed at school to remind myself (and others) that the class was non-negotiable and everyone respected that. It meant I had a couple of evenings a week where I wasn't working until the site manager came round rattling his keys, and my colleagues were used to my routine. Best of all, the school didn't collapse because I had a life outside work, and I wasn't quite so burnt out by the end of term!

Deputy head

● CASE STUDY

One particular success we had in schools was 'secret friends' – all staff names put in a hat (including caretaker/chef, etc.). Everyone randomly chose one and they had to spend two weeks secretly doing nice things for that person, for example leaving them a cuppa, paying a compliment, leaving a nice note in the register. Despite my ground rules of no money being spent, obviously there were a few who decided to 'break' this rule much to the disappointment of those who had obedient secret friends! The other little side effect was people generally being nicer and kinder to each other in order to throw people off the scent of the true identity of their secret friend. Two weeks later, secret friends were guessed and revealed. Much to my delight, every member of staff went on to do 'secret friends' with their own class, spreading the ethos of kindness and friendliness, and this really contributed to staff morale overall.

PSHE co-ordinator

❄ SOMETHING TO THINK ABOUT

You're probably already doing a lot of things that support the PSHE curriculum such as school council, visits and visitors, extra-curricular clubs and schemes like 'Rights Respecting Schools' and 'Walk to School'. It's worth spending some time just thinking about the consistency of the messages you're giving across these additional activities. Do they match up with the aims of your PSHE policy? Do they support the planned curriculum and enhance it? Are they trundling on as they have been for years and feel a little out of step with other aspects of school life? If so, think about how these activities can work more effectively. Perhaps school council processes need a shake up and meetings organised in a different way. Could meetings do with being more or less frequent to make them more meaningful? Do extra-curricular activities reflect the range of need at your school? Are there any that need to be rethought in terms of content or frequency? Do all key staff members (including external providers) know and understand the aims of your PSHE programme and are they able to bring out the elements in their activities?

Chapter Six

TAKING THE NEXT STEPS

Flying the flag for PSHE is not always easy. Finding space in a crowded curriculum in which the pressures for academic results can be overwhelming may feel like a constant battle, but placing PSHE at the heart of the school not only supports academic learning but will also help children deal with their world, both now and in the future. Surely our role as educators means that we are part of the village raising the child? We have a responsibility to support our young people and make sure they are ready for the next step of their lives.

PSHE continually needs to be changed slightly, to take account of the latest legislation and guidance, the needs of the pupils in your school and in reaction to work events, so it makes sense to build a support network. You may be lucky enough to have local authority support or networks and access to specialists within your local area, and it's worth making time to connect with others locally to share good practice.

If you do only one thing, make sure you join the PSHE Association, either as a personal member or through school. The PSHE Association campaigns for better PSHE and provides updates and teaching materials. Its Quality Mark puts resources through a rigorous assessment process to ensure that they adhere to the principles and practice of good PSHE teaching and learning, and it sends out email updates each time a new resource is added to its database. Being up to date is invaluable in making sure that you're teaching PSHE safely and accurately. The PSHE Association also runs training courses throughout the year and holds an annual conference that alternates between London and Leeds, which is worth attending.

Mentor-ADEPIS runs seminars throughout the country about all aspects of drug and alcohol education and also runs webinars: these are another reliable source of up-to-date information and advice.

Various companies run PSHE training throughout the country, but please check on the credentials of the company and its trainers. Encourage colleagues to take part in PSHE training too. If budgets are tight, think about how you could feed back to colleagues after a course or network meeting to ensure the right messages get through.

Social media provide a good way to network virtually with colleagues, to share resources and to ask questions. As already mentioned, there are various education Twitter hashtags, but if you search on Twitter for 'PSHE' or '#PSHE', you'll find accounts you can follow and discussion and debate about PSHE issues. Teachers often ask questions on specific lessons or problems and receive support and ideas from a range of teaching colleagues and other professionals.

The online *Times Educational Supplement* has a huge bank of resources, so if you need an assembly outline or some ideas for PSHE lessons, it's a good place to start. A word of caution, however: resources created by professional colleagues will have been created with their own schools in mind, so you will need to think about how the resource might work with your own school. Check carefully that the resource follows the PSHE Association's 'Ten Principles of PSHE Education' (in the Appendix). Sometimes the resources and lesson plans may spark ideas for your own practice. If you're looking for creative and imaginative display and lesson ideas, then Pinterest is another possible source of bright ideas.

Creating an action plan for PSHE

Creating an action plan for PSHE will help you focus on what you want your school to achieve and will help to keep PSHE in others' minds too. Ideally it should be part of the school development plan or whatever other process is used by your school to plan for progress.

Yes, it's another piece of paperwork to complete, but ensure that it works for you by making it really specific and meaningful. Too often, action plans for PSHE can be flabby and vague ('Continue to plan and teach PSHE') – how can you make the planning meaningful?

What do you want to achieve?

Think about where you are now and where you want to be with PSHE in two or three years' time. Consider some of the topics covered in this book and jot down some ideas. Involve other staff by asking them to think of what they would want for every child leaving your school. What qualities and experiences would you want the children to have? How can PSHE support you in promoting these? What are you doing now in terms of PSHE to support these goals? For example, if your colleagues feel that pupils need more learning on managing friendships in real life and online, then look at where you are now. Take into account behaviour records, feedback from staff, children's and parents' views, and other available data. Is your PSHE programme meaningful, relevant, age-appropriate, creative and aspirational? What could you do to give it a boost?

Break each step down into milestones along the way where you can stop and review progress and adapt targets, if necessary, depending on what is working and what isn't. There's no point in sticking rigidly to a set target if it turns out to be impossible to achieve or if you achieve it sooner than expected.

Setting targets

Long-term targets

A long-term target might be something like this:

> By [year], all children will have had at least six hours of teaching within the PSHE programme, which will include developing skills around managing friendships on- and offline (Reception to Year Six); and 50 per cent of parents and carers will have attended an e-safety course.

Milestones:

- By end of first year of plan, all children will have received at least three hours of teaching as above.

- Course on e-safety for parents and carers run as part of school induction. Evaluations at least 80 per cent 'good'.

Or another example of a target:

> There will be an annual Health Week in the spring term every year.

Milestones:

- Health Week dates built into school timetable for next three years.

- Information about Health Week available on school website, with posters in office.

Medium-term targets

This is an example of a medium-term target:

By end of school year, PSHE planning will include a module around managing friendships on- and offline for all KS2 pupils, and planning for KS1 will include simple assessments on feelings and managing friendships.

Milestones:

- PSHE lead has attended a course on teaching relationships and disseminated any ideas and materials to staff (via staff meeting) before end of term.

- Working party has developed a pack of six lessons for KS2 and these have been trialled (by end of year).

- A focus group of pupils has given feedback on the impact and experiences of the lessons.

- All teachers have trialled simple assessments in KS1 to monitor impact.

- Behaviour records have shown a drop in friendship problems. Midday staff are reporting that pupils are better able to manage any problems in the playground.

A different target might be this:

We will hold our first Health Week. Afterwards, we will evaluate what worked and what impact it had on children's learning.

Milestones:

- Health Week has been planned and run. A focus group has evaluated its impact.

- Staff have reported back on any further impacts of Health Week learning.

- End-of-year pupil and parent surveys each include two questions about Health Week and its impact.

Short-term targets

A short-term target might look like this:

Year Five will trial a module of six lessons concerning managing feelings, friendships (on- and offline) and assertiveness.

Milestones:

- Year Five staff have attended a short training session in school (on using the materials) and understand their roles.

- Year Five staff have taught the lessons and completed the assessments.

- Year Five staff have met to discuss what went well and what didn't, and identified any tweaks or changes before rolling out to Year Four and Year Six.

Another target might be:

We will set up a small working party to plan our first Health Week and this will meet once a fortnight from half-term.

Milestones:

Working-party members have been selected and invited by the Health Week contact teacher to an initial meeting.

Dates set in the diary for the rest of term. Room or space booked for meetings.

Item added to governors' agenda to enlist support.

Monitoring progress

Many schools use headings in a grid or spreadsheet to keep track of progress. If your school already uses a method that works well, use that one; otherwise, headings might include these:

- Long-term/medium-term/short-term objectives

- Baseline information

- What you plan to do

- Actions or milestones

- By whom

- Resources/budget

- Outcomes for children

Try where possible to make sure that targets are 'SMART' (specific, measurable, agreed-upon, relevant, time-based). Avoid vague generalisations such as 'PSHE will continue to be taught using the scheme of work' or 'Pupils will receive active and engaging PSHE lessons'.

In terms of reviewing PSHE teaching and learning itself, you could use the PSHE Association core themes to start planning:

- Health and wellbeing

- Relationships

- Living in the wider world – economic wellbeing and being a responsible citizen

Even if you're not in charge of leading PSHE in your school, it may still be worth making your own PSHE plan – not to create more work for yourself, but to sharpen your own focus. Such a plan may help you spot gaps in teaching and learning, and encourage you to step out of your comfort zone and to try out new activities and ways of working. You'll also spot overlaps with other subject areas and this will help when planning creative, practical lessons that really make a difference. Keep this book handy and refer to it if you need a bit of inspiration or simply a reminder of what works and why.

Somehow PSHE has found you: the onus is now on you to create experiences that will support pupils through life, both now and in the future. There is plenty of support out there for PSHE teachers, too, and simply by picking up this book you have started to connect with that community. Good luck on your PSHE journey.

Ten Principles of PSHE Education

Our ten principles underpin all of our work and guidance for teachers and schools. The PSHE Association has developed the following evidence-based principles of good practice in PSHE education:

1. Start where children and young people are: find out what they already know, understand, are able to do and are able to say. For maximum impact involve them in the planning of your PSHE education programme.

2. Plan a 'spiral programme' which introduces new and more challenging learning, while building on what has gone before, which reflects and meets the personal developmental needs of the children and young people.

3. Take a positive approach which does not attempt to induce shock or guilt but focuses on what children and young people can do to keep themselves healthy and safe and to lead happy and fulfilling lives.

4. Offer a wide variety of teaching and learning styles within PSHE education, with an emphasis on interactive learning and the teacher as facilitator.

5. Provide information which is realistic and relevant and which reinforces positive social norms.

6. Encourage young people to reflect on their learning and the progress they have made, and to transfer what they have learned

to say and to do from one school subject to another, and from school to their lives in the wider community.

7. Recognise that the PSHE education programme is just one part of what a school can do to help a child to develop the knowledge, skills, attitudes and understanding they need to fulfil their potential. Link the PSHE education programme to other whole-school approaches, to pastoral support, and provide a setting where the responsible choice becomes the easy choice. Encourage staff, families and the wider community to get involved.

8. Embed PSHE education within other efforts to ensure children and young people have positive relationships with adults, feel valued and where those who are most vulnerable are identified and supported.

9. Provide opportunities for children and young people to make real decisions about their lives, to take part in activities which simulate adult choices and where they can demonstrate their ability to take responsibility for their decisions.

10. Provide a safe and supportive learning environment where children and young people can develop the confidence to ask questions, challenge the information they are offered, draw on their own experience, express their views and opinions and put what they have learned into practice in their own lives.

Reproduced with kind permission from the PSHE Association[1]

---

1   PSHE Association (2014, updated 2018) *Ten Principles of Effective PSHE Education.* London: PSHE Association.

Printed in Great Britain
by Amazon